Books & Products by Olivia McIvor

The Business of Kindness:
Creating Work Environments Where People Thrive

The Kindness Journal:
Twelve Ways to Bring More Kindness Into Your Life & Work

The Kindness Cards:
80 Tools to Help You Build a Kinder Workplace

Four Generations, One Workplace:
Sharing in the Information Age

The Ah-Ha Cards:
Generational Reminders that Aid Communication

Turning Compassion into Action:
A Movement Toward Taking Responsibility

Compassion in Action Cards
Change the world one person, one action at a time

For more information on workplace and personal development products visit: OLIVIA**MCIVOR**.com

To inquire about quantity discounts please call 604-913-0649.
To order direct visit www.fairwinds-press.com

Turning Compassion into Action

Turning Compassion into Action

A Movement Toward Taking Responsibility

Olivia McIvor

FairWinds Press
Vancouver, BC

FairWinds Press publishes works that help create positive change in our world. We pay attention to our environment as our core values influence every decision we make. We proudly donate a percentage of our profits to charitable organizations. Our books are printed on long lasting acid free paper. When available we choose paper that has been manufactured by environmentally responsible processes. These may include using trees grown in sustainable forests, incorporating recycled paper, reduced energy harvesting as well as the absence of chlorine bleach.

FairWinds Press
PO Box 668, Lions Bay BC CANADA , V0N2E0
Tel: 604-913-0649   www.fairwinds-press.com

All rights reserved. No part of this publication may be reproduced, distributed, or transmitted in any form or by any means, including photocopying, recording, or other electronic or mechanical methods without the prior written permission of the publisher, except in cases of brief quotations for critical reviews. For permission requests write to the publisher, addressed "Attention: Permissions" at the address above. Although the author and publisher have made every effort to ensure that the information in this book was correct at press time, the author and publisher do not assume and hereby disclaim any liability to any party for any loss, damage, or disruption caused by errors or omissions, whether such errors or omissions result from negligence, accident, or any other cause.

Permissions:

"Charter for Compassion" by Karen Armstrong, copyright © Karen Armstrong, used by permission of the author.

Quotation from Sadiqa N. Reynolds, used by permission of the author.

Narrative stories and conversations within this text are used with permission of those authors.

Scarboro Missions Interfaith department, "The Golden Rule", from the Golden Rule Poster, used by permission of the author.

Copyright © 2013 Olivia McIvor
Printed in the United States of America.

Library and Archives Canada Cataloguing in Publication

McIvor, Olivia, 1959-
    Turning compassion into action : a movement toward taking responsibility / Olivia McIvor.

Includes bibliographical references and index.
Issued also in electronic format.

ISBN 978-0-9881081-0-3
    1. Compassion--Case studies. 2. Conduct of life--Case studies.
3. Responsibility--Case studies. I. Title.

BJ1475.M45 2013   361.7   C2013-902141-8

First Edition   15 14 13 12 11 10   9 8 7 6 5 4 3 2 1

Contents

Dedication		xi
Foreword by Erie Chapman		xiii
Introduction		xv
Imagery Used		xvii
Chapter 1	A Commitment	1.
Chapter 2	A Devotion	21.
Chapter 3	A Science	49.
Chapter 4	Compassionate Optimism	75.
Chapter 5	Compassionate Purpose	129.
Chapter 6	Compassionate Belonging	163.
Chapter 7	Compassionate Presence	201.
Chapter 8	A Movement Forward	253.
A Contemplative Guide		261.
Sources		275.
Index		289.
With Gratitude		295.
About the Author		299.

x

Dedication

This book cannot be dedicated solely to one person or event. Compassion is an alive and awake presence. It is in everything we say and don't say. It is in everything we do and don't do. It is everything we are and everything we will be. From sunrise to sunset and all that remains in-between. May we all be worthy of such a friend.

Foreword

Olivia McIvor has written an important book about the most important energy we know: Love—and the compassion that flows from it. Compassion lives at the center of our humanity and McIvor affirms this with eloquent language, concepts that catch in the heart, and powerful stories that paint pictures of the Love we want on this earth.

If compassion is a naturally occurring energy, why do we have to "learn" it? Can it really be taught? McIvor, with memorable phrasing, helps us recognize that compassion is better "caught than taught."

How?

If you want to practice compassion in ways that will change your life as well as the lives of those around you, read every word of *Turning Compassion into Action* and then read the book again and again. As you merge McIvor's thoughts into yours and practice them you will find that she has handed you a rich gift: a way to live as you have always wanted to by practicing the compassion that is your highest self.

McIvor has experienced so many heartrending stories of her own that it is easy to see why she understands this work well enough to write about it. Her parables help us "catch" Love's energy. The stories she tells, built on the concepts she teaches, will move you to action.

Olivia McIvor has devoted her life to helping us appreciate compassion's power in our lives. Now, flowing from her life experience, her workshops, and her research, comes this book. It is as beautiful as is her heart.

Is there any more meaningful thing you can do than to read this? Yes. You can do what she asks of you: take responsibility for practicing compassion more radically than you have ever done before.

Is there any more important way to live?

Erie Chapman, M.T.S., J.D.
Author, *Radical Loving Care*
Past President and CEO, Riverside Methodist Hospitals and Baptist Hospital System

Introduction

Modest doubt is call'd the beacon of the wise.

William Shakespeare

I would like to think I started this book with modest doubt. Yet, after completion, I have concluded that it is closer to a humble, pensive doubt. As to the wise part, I don't imagine myself to be wise, or to truly know the answer to the question that begged this book to be written: What is compassion?

Perhaps compassion is not an ill-defined word to you; if so, you are fortunate. For myself, I found I needed to join with other perspectives. Over the course of a year I asked for, and received, poetry, thoughts, and stories on compassion from hundreds of individuals who wrote to me about their perceptions and experiences.

This book is also imbued with the research I have garnered from my workshops on kindness and compassion in the workplace. I have spoken to thousands of participants and, in these workshops, they have shared thoughts and stories that have stayed with me, colored my thinking, and changed my outlook.

As a consequence, this book is not penned exclusively by me; it is a collaborative effort that reflects the wisdom and compassion of others in its pages. I have come away humbled by the generosity and honesty of all who have shared their stories and perceptions, and I have tried to be the wiser for their sharing.

The beloved children's book author and illustrator Beatrix Potter once wrote, "There is something delicious about writing the first words of a story. You never quite know where they'll take you." When I started to explore this nebulous word, compassion, I had no idea where it would take me. The journey has been rich, at times surprising, and always rewarding.

With gratitude,

Imagery Used

The original image used in this text is as multidimensional as it is creative. It allows for specific features to be highlighted in order to signify each chapter's message. This image illustrates the infinite and interwoven fabric of our lives.

The image used in *A Commitment* illustrates two toned hearts interlinked and committed to the same common body. When we join together in commitment we are infinitely more powerful to the pursuit of the common good for all.

The image used in *A Devotion* illustrates a solitary devotion to one's own values and beliefs. The ultimate quest for devotion is a heart devoted to love and compassion.

The image used in *A Science* illustrates our solar system and the infinite continuum as science pursues its quest to find proof to substantial universal questions.

Chapter 1

A Commitment

*Unless commitment is made,
there are only promises and hopes; but no plans.*

Peter F. Drucker

No one has ever 'become poor' by giving.

Anne Frank, diary of Anne Frank

"Blue, red, yellow..." I enunciated each word slowly as I threw the primary-colors up into the air. The launch of each balloon was greeted with beaming faces. We giggled like schoolgirls as we tried to keep the fragile, airy balls from hitting the ground.

That crisp winter afternoon, I shared a childish delight with ten women residents at Mother Teresa's Home for the Destitute and Dying in New Delhi. We blew up balloons and forgot about that long condemnation of a name for a time. Oneness comes naturally when a common aim is shared, even if it is as simple and humble as keeping balloons aloft in the air.

While I sat on the ground, resting for a moment, Mother Placid came to stand next to me. The humble white cotton sari she wore wrapped around her in layers; the signature blue trim of the Missionaries of Charity lined its bottom folds in what seemed like an endless circle that encompassed and drew us all in.

Suddenly, she bent down, leaned into me, and whispered in her accented Indian English, "All the residents want is love and affection. In return, they will give you back love and affection." Looking at me as though looking through me, she continued, "This is giving and receiving—compassion is witnessed in the middle."

We all experience moments in our lives that compel us to think, feel, and eventually act and live in the world differently. Sometimes, these moments are thrust upon us; and sometimes, like a balloon bobbing in the air, they seem random. They may even seem more noteworthy in retrospect because we were not in quest of them, but rather, it is as though they sought us out—to call us into action and out of our complacency.

I was gifted with two of these moments, seemingly random in nature and then coming together as though they were destined to collaborate with one another. They brought me to this decayed, and yet stunningly beautiful, corner of India as part of a two-year search and exploration that took me to other parts of the world and brought me home.

That first moment came to me when a gentleman in a blue maintenance uniform shared a story.

Light Bulbs and Compassion

I had just asked the audience to share their own stories of compassion when the hefty man in the blue uniform rose from his seat at the back of the room. "I didn't come here to learn about compassion," he said. "I came here to change light bulbs and mop floors. That's what my job description says."

I wasn't quite sure where he was heading. Was he stating his dislike of the two-hour kick-off session of the "Contagious Kindness: Putting Values into Action" program his healthcare organization had just launched? Or was he going to share a story?

The gentleman continued as though in a confessional booth, struggling at first to find the right words. "I came here to work for six months to get back on my feet after losing my job. I have now been here for over 20 years. Every day for years, as I mopped floors and changed light bulbs, I would mind my own business as I silently watched the staff and volunteers do their jobs. I would observe how they approached patients and families, how they said some small comment or touched people gently. I would see how they looked into their eyes—never saying a word, or how they made a simple gesture that meant a lot, like a smile."

He stalled for a minute. I thought he was concluding his sharing, but he eventually found his words. "Then, one day, an elderly man in his eighties walked through the front doors of the hospital and stood frozen in the middle of the foyer looking around. I thought to myself that maybe I should go over and check on him as he appeared lost. Lots of people get lost in a hospital, but he looked anxious and even scared.

"I took my mop and I hurriedly cleaned my way over to where he was and asked if I could help. 'My wife has arrived by ambulance and I don't know where to find her,' the elderly man told me, shaking. 'If you go over to reception they will tell you where she is,' I said and pointed him toward the desk. He walked over and stood in line impatiently waiting his turn.

"After his turn he walked back out to the center of the entrance hall and he froze again, and I said to myself, 'Not again.' So, I walked over to him and he had this look that told me he wasn't okay. Sure, he had found out she was on the seventh floor, but he didn't know where the elevators were. So I said, 'If you go down that hallway and turn left …' then I thought to myself that he looked so upset that maybe I should just walk him to the elevators."

I could well imagine this scene. I have conducted many events in hospital settings and care facilities and have found myself navigating endless hallways, absorbed in the hurried milieu of busy workers on task to get a job done—not to mention the array of concerned families and friends arriving and departing, and the ill patients wandering the floors.

The storyteller moved further into sharing his account and we, his audience, sat unsure of when we could exhale, as we awaited the outcome of his narrative. "When we got there, I thought... maybe I should just press the seventh floor button for him... well, I am here anyways—may as well ride up there and make sure he finds the nurses' station, as those hallways are confusing.

"When the elevator doors opened I showed him where the station was, but something inside of me said to wait, so I did. The man found out his wife's room number and started to walk down the hallway and, once again, froze partway down. He ran back toward me and I said, 'Is everything okay? What's wrong?'

"In a shaky voice, and near tears, he told me he had been in such a hurry to get into the hospital that he had parked his car in front of a restricted zone and they would tow his car if he didn't move it. And that is when I got it. I really got it. I said to him, 'Give me your keys. I will go move your car, park it, and bring the keys back to you. You go take care of your wife.'"

I looked around the room. I saw hands quietly wiping away surreptitious tears. I heard people shuffling in their seats. The man in the blue maintenance uniform finished his account. "After all of those years of watching other people hand out compassion, I finally understood how to do it myself, how it is part of my job, and that I am responsible to be as compassionate as the primary caregivers are."

I had to take a deep breath to gather myself before I could respond. And, even as I did so, I recognized that this was a defining moment for me—that I would remember where I was and what had been said and how it had changed a viewpoint of mine. Not just any viewpoint, but a deeply held understanding and conviction of something I had thought I knew and didn't have to unlearn.

We tend to believe that we add new knowledge to old learning and, miraculously, we keep growing and expanding our wisdom. But, in that instant, I realized I needed to unlearn something in order to replace it with a new learning. I had always believed that compassion was something to be taught; but, in hearing the man with the blue maintenance uniform speak, it came to me: what if compassion was something that could be caught? What if it was something that could be transmitted organically and not by rote?

It was only after I'd spent time thinking about the man's story that the second random moment brought itself to my attention and reminded me that it had been waiting in the wings.

Eight months earlier, I had attended a meeting with the organizational development team responsible for the Contagious Kindness program I was writing for a healthcare client and which was to eventually be the kick-off event attended by the man in the blue maintenance uniform.

Betty, the leader in charge of the development of the training program, made a profoundly simple comment. She said, "Compassion is not a checklist."

Her comment emerged out of frustration as she searched for a way to articulate what she was thinking in and around this nebulous word. I left the meeting, got on an airplane home, and felt like a dog with a bone.

From Candles to a Koan

As many reading this may know, my first book is titled, *The Business of Kindness: Creating Work Environments Where People Thrive.* I have had the privilege of sharing its message for many years with a wide range of clients through consulting, speaking engagements, as well as training and development programs.

In addition, my Contagious Kindness and Compassion in Action programs are tailored, licensed programs that have supported well over 25,000 employees in taking personal responsibility in the workplace: to be the change they want to see—one person and one action at a time.

With this volume of individuals participating in a range of related programs—and countless others crossing my path—my outreach is expansive, my research is current, and my approach is hands-on. I have been both vulnerable to, and inspired by, the many thought-provoking questions, profound insights, and inspirational stories participants so generously shared.

They made me realize that we have the ability to blow out a candle or even a group of candles—that is, we can quench or avoid bright moments that call for our attention. But a fire—that is different. No one person on her own is capable of putting out a fire when individual flames unite. I was sensing that candles had been lit for me, and now these candles were morphing into a blaze. Once I realized that, I had a bright and burning desire to address the questions that had found their way to me, and I understood that I alone could not address them.

By force of habit, and due to years of management training, I moved speedily into auto-drive problem solving. "Okay, Olivia, first identify the problem. Then conduct a root cause analysis, brainstorm solutions, and develop an action plan."

I found compassion resisted being analyzed like this. But if it could not be condensed into a working list with checks and balances, how could it be measured, quantified, or qualified? Unknowingly, the man in the blue maintenance uniform had inspired a tablet of questions I yearned to answer and an ambiguity I embraced.

Questions are one of my forms of meditation, similar to a Koan—a Japanese discipline where short paradoxical questions are posed by Zen masters to weaken the persistent logical mind so the insightful, intuitive mind can take over. Asking provocative questions has been an important driver throughout my life; they galvanize me to work through puzzling issues at multiple layers and levels.

So I abandoned the traditional business model of problem solving and began to ask questions. Is compassion like a virus—can it be caught and spread around? Is it contagious? Do we learn how to be compassionate through surveillance and observing how others model the behavior? Can this noun be turned into a verb?

Betty's comment felt so right: the intangible and profound qualities that compassion encompasses are so much more than a checklist.

The Space Between Us

My questions reached out and gathered in others. Through my work in profit and non-profit sectors, I had become aware of a widening space, a gap between colleagues, which spills into our personal settings. Abraham Lincoln was known as a kind and compassionate man who, when he didn't like someone, would say, "I must get to know him better."

Unfortunately, in today's culture, we tend to be doing the opposite. We tend to turn away rather than toward one another. We are creating a space between us. It may be caused by social and personal constructs, but the net effect is the same. We are becoming strangers to one another—lost in a sea of people, places, and possessions.

Mother Placid had offered a profound possibility when she said, "Compassion is witnessed in the middle." My observation of the growing space between us led me to ask, "Can compassion offer a way for us to change the space between us? To thrive, not just survive? Can compassion transform this isolating space?"

The Hidden Picture

I liken my queries about compassion to gazing at a "hidden objects" picture. Defocus your gaze and, if you do so long enough, hidden images appear within the picture and the original fades into the background.

My journey has called me to a similar process: to defocus my attention—to let go of the picture as I think I see it, allowing my gaze and heart to soften—so that I may open my mind to what has been heretofore unseen, unnoticed, and perhaps even misunderstood.

Compassion, in the dictionary, has been defined as "a feeling of distress and pity for the suffering or misfortune of another, often including the desire to alleviate it." Various other dictionary versions reference compassion as, "to suffer with" or "a feeling of deep sympathy and sorrow for another who is stricken by misfortune." Language such as this may inspire a fear of compassion—a fear of being engulfed by pessimism or despair.

But look beyond the definitions in the foreground—let the background come to the fore—and something more is found. In Latin, the prefix "com" means "with"; combine that with "passion" and so it is with passion that I ask you to move forward with me.

A Quest

I set about on an exploration of compassion. Over the course of two years, I travelled, researched, taught, worked, and wrote. I volunteered in my community. I went to Morocco to volunteer in an orphanage with 250 children under the age of 6.

I also traveled to New Delhi, India, to work at Mother Teresa's Home for the Destitute and Dying run by her order, Missionaries of Charity. These blessed Sisters offer a home for 165 of India's "poorest of the poor"—those abandoned by family and society, most considered "untouchable" within the culture. The care offered ranged from end-of-life to ministering to every manner of physical, mental, and emotional ailment.

> If you deny yourself commitment, what can you do with your life?
>
> Harvey Fierstein

I have no medical background and when I arrived, I suddenly felt ill-equipped; most of the other volunteers had some form of healthcare background. I shared my apprehension with one of my fellow volunteers the night before our placement began. "What good can a consultant do?" I whispered in a voice burdened with an unfamiliar heaviness.

Heather, a nurse from Pennsylvania who had served six years earlier at this location and was familiar with the setup, replied without hesitation, "Olivia, they don't need medical attention as much as they need compassion."

She knew nothing of my personal mission to search out compassion, discover its meaning, and find it in action. That is when I knew I had come to the right place.

After returning home, I began to ask others what compassion meant to them. No one was embarrassed, nor did they take offence at my questions; rather, they were as excited as I was to explore where they sat within this blessed space of grace and how accountable they felt to act upon their own understanding—and, even more so, what was going on for them between their heart and mind while delivering benevolence to another.

In so many of the discussions I had with others, the conclusion reached was that acting with compassion had a tremendously positive impact on both the giver and the receiver—it was as though an embracing, inclusive circle was created, much like the signature blue trim of Mother Placid's sari.

Under the safe umbrella of compassionate dialogue, we asked why individuals would avoid reaching out across communities and workplaces. Fear seemed to be the common thread. Fear of making a mistake—of saying or doing the wrong thing. Fear of awakening and triggering one's personal past. Fear of the recipient's reaction or non-reaction. Fear of being the first to step into the unknown.

Granite Floor Teachable Moments

I am fully aware that my characterization of compassion may not be everyone's, and therein lies the rub and the blessing of our unique perspectives. For me, putting language to this influential and ubiquitous word came in a multitude of profound ways while volunteering at Mother Teresa's Home.

A gray granite floor became my most significant teacher more than once. Moments of clarity came during weekly wash days full of clothing, sheets, and towels. Alongside the residents—those to whom we were there to be of service—we volunteers would kneel on an inflexible and cold granite floor, plunging our hands in soapy water buckets to roughly scrub the laundry on manual washboards. Jointly we would move each item from vast buckets of water until the water ran as clear as rain and then we would team up and hand-wring each piece of cloth so we could hang it on the clothesline on the rooftop for the afternoon breeze to dry.

Compassion was my mentor.

In every chore there arose an opportunity to administer an action using my hands and my mind to figure out how to best get it done. What I soon uncovered was a need to ask myself how I was bringing my heart to my duties while using my hands. How do I administer compassion in the wake of the chaos and hurriedness to complete the tasks to which I was assigned? How do I do this under the watchful eyes of the Sisters to whom cleanliness was paramount—and rightly so, as you cannot have close to one hundred women cloistered in a couple of rooms and not be mindful of the importance of hygiene.

In every new and repeated task I thought of the thousands of workers in a multitude of sectors to whom I have had the privilege of speaking at events and conferences, and facilitating in training programs. I thought of how easy it is to disconnect from the compassionate side of customer or patient service in order to complete the task-oriented side of business. When the crazy making of the day takes hold and all we can think about is completing our tasks, do we stop and take inventory of why we are really there?

In order to hold myself accountable and to combine my work with compassionate care, I reminded myself daily that the residents were not an interruption of my work duties, but the reason for them.

What Does Compassion Mean to You?

As I continued to search for the deeper meaning of compassion and its role in our lives, I invited others to join me through a call for contributions. People were to address one simple, yet infinitely complex question: What does compassion mean to you?

I wanted to begin a conversation and to listen; I wanted the contributors to be authentic and sincere; and I hoped that the readers of this book would have their hearts aroused and awakened—that they would consider, question, and reflect on how what they read might align with their personal values.

Most importantly, I hoped to offer something that helps us along our way, so that, when we breathe our last breath, we know we have lived a good life: a life that matters, a life built consciously, a life of shared humanity, of knowing that we are all in this together as a global community.

As I wrote and thought, as I listened and discussed, I began to see that compassion encompasses something greater than all of us—that it brings us plenitude and gifts. Gradually, the shape of this book made itself clear to me—that compassion lives and thrives in optimism, purpose, belonging, and presence; that it springs from a great spiritual well; and that, nebulous though compassion is, its fragility, strength, and beauty can be expressed in scientific terms.

I hope you find something in this book that speaks to you. I hope you find inspiration for your own commitment and quest. And, most of all, I hope you savor the stories and feel as though each contributor has welcomed you to their kitchen table to sip tea and share a sweet conversation with you.

Chapter 2

A Devotion

The need for devotion to something outside ourselves is even more profound than the need for companionship.
If we are not to go to pieces or wither away, we must have some purpose in life; for no man can live for himself alone.

Ross Paramenter, Anthropologist

True strength lies in submission which permits one to dedicate his life, through devotion, to something beyond himself.

Henry Miller

On a December day, Nancy went into labor and, a week later, took her son home from the neonatal intensive care unit. She wrote, "According to the doctor there were three possible outcomes for our son: he could die, he could be severely mentally damaged, or he could be a year behind in school."

With little warning, we all may find ourselves at a threshold. We must take a step and then another, and a journey has begun. Nancy's journey started when her son Chris was born with cerebral palsy.

> As my son progressed through the numerous appointments, assessments, treatments, and therapies in his early years, my marriage became strained and eventually broke under the stress. I struggled to understand the nagging question, 'Why was this happening?'
> By the time Chris turned seven, I had blamed myself for the past seven years—looking for something I had done

> wrong during the pregnancy. Maybe if I had taken better care of myself, worked less shift work, said more prayers...

As I read Nancy's account, I was humbled by her honesty and vulnerability. Have we not all asked at some point, "Why is this happening?" Have we not all doubted and blamed ourselves? Faced with a challenge that calls for our best, faced with a journey that may seem daunting, we may choose to shrug and turn away when there are other choices beckoning our hearts and souls. Nancy did not have that luxury. Like any parent, she was, quite simply, the loving mother of a child who needed her care.

> I remember a friend said to me one day, "We are given the 'special ones' because we have the strength to care." And with that sage piece of advice I gradually started to understand that there was a reason *why* I was going through this experience of raising a child with a disability.
>
> I started to look at life differently. Life was not a struggle but a challenge to be matched with the courage to learn and the strength to believe.

A Profound Human Calling

Few of us are called as Nancy has been—and, yet, we can all be as equally committed and caring. We can all be as devoted.

Latin in its origin, the word "devotion" is derived from "devovere," which, when broken apart, means "de" (which is "to") and "votum" (meaning "vow")—making the very essence of the language stand for making a vow or a promise to something outside of oneself. Listen to Nancy:

> The common cliché often said without contemplation—"everything happens for a reason"—was becoming clearer to me. A shift in my perspective was as if a whole new way of "knowing" opened my way of being. A fresh way of seeing and acting was now before me.
>
> As I watched my son grow and develop, I too began to grow and develop. Expecting the usual, I had been given an unusual way to see the world through my son's eyes—his special way of perceiving the world and his unique ways of interacting with others.
>
> My son had to work for everything in his daily life: he struggled to eat and drink, to hold his head up, to crawl, to toilet train, to walk, and talk. But, one thing he did not have to struggle to do was to smile and to laugh.

The Epicenter

To be a more loving and compassionate human being has always been at the hearthstone, has been part of a mother's nurture and a father's love, has been there to warm us on chilly nights, to assist in making sense of famine and war, and, most importantly, to teach us to contribute to the well-being of our tribes.

Devoted care of another is a profound human calling and one that we all are responsible to offer and receive as an active member of a larger clan.

Whether one studies philosophy, sees life from a spiritual perspective, or embraces one of the major faith-based traditions, I believe compassion lives at the epicenter—it is one of the core values or virtues of the majority of secular and non-secular beliefs.

From my own experience and understanding, I would be hard pressed to find any individual perspective or faith that does not express the responsibility to act with compassion as a founding core value.

The tenets of Buddhism remind us that it is not what happens to us so much as how we respond to our own suffering and the suffering of others. His Holiness the Dalai Lama advises us, "If you want others to be happy, practice compassion. If you want to be happy, practice compassion."

Nancy's story shares that with us a hundredfold.

A Lifelong Quest

I think I was no more than five years old when I went shopping one day with my mother down the main street in our little farming community. She went into the hairdresser's salon to have her hair cut. After a short time, I slipped out the door and wandered down the block. I came to a small church on a street lined with large trees budding white cherry blossoms, and went inside.

Even though my mother did not know where I was, I sat patiently and unafraid in the hush and quiet of the little church, waiting for her to arrive. I felt as though this was where I was supposed to be. I had not been raised in a religious household, but there was something inside me wanting to be in quiet contemplation even at this young age.

During my high school years, I attended further to this spiritual yearning. Madeline introduced me to Mormonism, Lori to Bahai, and Kami to Hinduism. Each week, my mother never knew which service I would be attending. Her belief was that, as long as you were happy and were taught to be a good person, there was no wrong in attending any or all.

This spiritual questing has also shaped my adult life. I have meditated in the ruins of Machu Picchu; sat in solitude in the ninth-century Buddhist Borobudur Temple in Indonesia; climbed the vortex mountains of Sedona, Arizona; bowed in the Hassan II Mosque in Casablanca; soaked my feet at sunset in the Ganges River during the Puja Ceremony in Rishikesh; sat in ceremony in sweat lodges in Canada;

and applied holy water in the Notre Dame Cathedral in Paris.

When I realized one day that I knew little about Judaism, I promptly enrolled in a course so I could learn. After traveling to Morocco, I returned home with an English translation of the Qur'an and signed up for a 30-day study course with three scholars during Ramadan so I could find answers to questions my journey had inspired.

In time, I found my sentiments mirrored that of Chief Si'ahl, who is better known as Chief Seattle, the 19th-century Native American Elder after whom the city of Seattle, Washington, was named. In a speech given during the 1854 land treaty, he said, "This we know: all things are connected. Like the blood which unites one family, all things are connected. Our God is the same God whose compassion is equal for all."

As an adult who holds a reverence for the deeply held beliefs and convictions of others, I believe and hold true that compassion is deep-rooted in our humanity—that it is a wellspring that may sustain and guide us in all we do.

A Circle and a Verb

When I opened Kam Wa's email, his first remark read, "Compassion is a verb." I smiled, for his thoughts so mirrored my own. Compassion does not live unless it is put into practice—unless it is made into a verb.

I liken compassion to three intersecting circles in order for it to manifest into action. One circle represents how I feel, how I can empathize with you. The second circle is how I think, how I understand your point of view and perceptions. The third circle, holding the three together, is the action inspired by how I think and feel. It is the element that binds and holds the circles because I am motivated to act on your behalf and for a higher purpose.

Kam Wa wrote to me from Hong Kong: "[Compassion] must involve action and not just mere thoughts in the mind. If I could be of help to someone in need, or what I do could benefit him or her in any particular way, I'd consider the act a form of compassion. The act in itself need not be anything grand. It could be a kind word, an empathetic ear, a genuine smile, or giving a hand to somebody. Compassion is something given without the slightest hope of having any good returns. It originates from the truthful heart and conscience."

His words remind me of how many times people who do heroic deeds say afterwards that they weren't being heroes—they were simply doing what they felt called upon to do. On September 11, colleagues desperately tried to help each other out of the burning twin towers. They said they didn't try to save themselves, they tried to save each other. They had no thought of any return. In their selfless devotion to another's welfare, they were acting from the truth within their hearts.

The Golden Rule

In offering my thoughts, I draw on my experience and reading, and most importantly, on what I have learned from contributors like Kam Wa and Nancy and those who have participated in my workshops and conferences. I have been affected by the latter in a profound way. In

> Do to others what you would have them do to you.
>
> The Golden Rule

countless discussions, these participants have repeatedly brought forward The Golden Rule. It never used to be in my materials, but has migrated there by virtue of its astonishing persistence and appearance over the years.

The Golden Rule holds that we should treat others as we would like them to treat us. This simple, yet universal, maxim translates across gender, culture, age, beliefs, and economic status.

Containing oral law, the sacred Rabbinic Judaism text of the Talmud reads, "When a person does a good deed when he or she didn't have to, God looks down and smiles and says, 'For this moment alone it was worth creating the world.'"

Georgina's husband was in the final stages of ALS (also known as Lou Gehrig's disease) and needed to be tube-fed at every meal. Georgina, an elementary school teacher and sole income provider, would drive home during her lunch hour to take care of her husband and then hurry back to work.

Her fellow teachers brought The Golden Rule to life during her time of need. For eight months, they placed homemade full-family meals in the school fridge every Tuesday and Thursday for her to take home. Georgina says her co-workers became her family and that they got her through the toughest year of her life. She says, "I wouldn't have made it without them."

The Golden Rule brings grace, and through its practice, we may understand that there is no true separation between our neighbors, families, and colleagues and ourselves. We may understand that showing devotion is as simple as the offer of a homemade meal.

A Global Compass

Scarboro Missions, located in Toronto, Canada, understands the universal significance of The Golden Rule. The society is dedicated to supporting the interfaith dialogue movement. They have set out The Golden Rule as it is expressed in 13 different world religions and traditions and have generously granted me permission to share these time-honored messages.

As you read through each version below, take a moment to reflect; each is a little different in its language. Indeed, I advocate putting aside the relationship to any particular affiliation and only concentrating on the message itself. One way to do this is to cover up the actual name of the faith: only read the statement. I invite you to take note of words or phrases that may particularly resonate with you and your own beliefs.

In alphabetical order, they read :

- Bahai Faith: "Lay not on any soul a load that you would not wish to be laid upon you, and desire not for anyone the things you would not desire for yourself." —Baha'u'llah, Gleanings

- Buddhism: "Treat not others in ways that you yourself would find hurtful." —The Buddha, Udana-Varga 5.18

- Christianity: "In everything, do to others as you would have them do to you; for this is the law and the prophets." —Jesus, Matthew 7:12

- Confucianism: "One word which sums up the basis of all good conduct...loving-kindness. Do not do to others what you do not want done to yourself." —Confucius, Analects 15.23

- Hinduism: "This is the sum of duty: do not do to others what would cause pain if done to you." —Mahabharata 5:1517

- Islam: "Not one of you truly believes until you wish for others what you wish for yourself." —The Prophet Muhammad, Hadith

- Jainism: "One should treat all creatures in the world as one would like to be treated." —Mahavira, Sutrakritanga 1.11.33

- Judaism: "What is hateful to you, do not do to your neighbour. This is the whole Torah; all the rest is commentary. Go and learn it." —Hillel, Talmud, Shabbath 31a

- Native Spirituality: "We are as much alive as we keep the earth alive." —Chief Dan George

- Sikhism: "I am a stranger to no one; and no one is a stranger to me. Indeed, I am a friend to all." —Guru Granth Sahib, p.1299

- Taoism: "Regard your neighbour's gain as your own gain and your neighbour's loss as your own loss." —Lao Tzu, T'ai Shang Kan Ying P'ien, 213-218

- Unitarianism: "We affirm and promote respect for the interdependent web of all existence of which we are a part." —Unitarian principle

- Zoroastrianism: "Do not do unto others whatever is injurious to yourself." —Shayast-na-Shayast 13.29

The Golden Rule is a natural moral compass that spans time and culture. It has the capacity to act as our guide should we stray off course, and to gently pull us back to our true north; the true north of who we are and how we would want to treat others.

A Reciprocal Design

The Golden Rule is also reciprocal in its intent. Reciprocity is created when one positive action generates another positive action and then the cycle continues—a succession of compassionate words and actions begets compassionate words and actions.

I am not sure there is really much else needed in the way of a code to live by. Imagine how commerce would be changed if this concept of compassionate reciprocity were applied. Or consider how family and community dynamics might be altered as historical kin issues and disputes were resolved more readily. Our communities at large, where the majority of people are strangers to one another, would come together in neighborhoods.

I ask workshop participants to contemplate questions such as, "If you applied your version of The Golden Rule, would you have handled a situation differently?" "If compassionate reciprocity were practiced by everyone in your workplace or family, how would that change it?"

I learned a contemplative practice called Just Like Me that I have used for years and that has always helped me set my compass. It is a form of devotion that can be done anywhere, anytime, and any place. Its words are reflective of The Golden Rule. Choose a person who needs your compassion. He or she could be family, friend, a co-worker, or even a stranger—maybe just someone you glimpsed while out walking or on the bus. Repeat the following phrase slowly to yourself as you stay centered on the individual and send them loving-kindness:

- Just like me, this person is seeking happiness (or joy or love) in his or her life.
- Just like me, this person is feeling sad (or lonely or is in grief).
- Just like me, this person is learning and doing the best he or she can.

Fill in the statement or create one that is appropriate to the situation. I have given examples above, but create what intuitively works for you. The simple beauty of this exercise is that judgment falls away and what springs to the surface is the stark realization that everyone is fighting a hard battle in some regard.

I believe that when we practice The Golden Rule or an exercise such as Just Like Me, we practice a form of devotion. We make a promise to something outside of ourselves.

A Global Compassion Movement

In 2008, Karen Armstrong, author and subject-matter expert on the role of religion in the modern world, won the TED prize as an individual who had made a substantial global impact. The award is accompanied by a financial endowment that allows its recipient to make "one wish to change the world." Armstrong knew immediately that her one wish was to be the creation of the Charter for Compassion, a founding document to inspire a global movement using the doctrine of The Golden Rule as its guiding principle.

Her ambition: bring together the wisdom of notable individuals from the secular and non-secular traditions, as well as solicit input from thousands of individuals via a multilingual website to create the charter. Submissions from across the world were received, read, and considered as the final document was crafted.

By November 2009, the Charter for Compassion was ready to launch in institutions, mosques, churches, temples, schools, and non-profits. As an online document, it has been translated into over 30 languages in order to reach the world. Tens of thousands of people have signed it.

The Charter expresses the ideal that The Golden Rule can be the dynamic force underlying the actions of individuals and organizations. The aim of the Charter is to transcend those dogmas that no longer serve and to awaken the essence of The Golden Rule in all of us. As you read through its message, note how it rouses your sensibilities to what is good and right.

Charter for Compassion

The principle of compassion lies at the heart of all religious, ethical, and spiritual traditions, calling us always to treat all others as we wish to be treated ourselves. Compassion impels us to work tirelessly to alleviate the suffering of our fellow creatures, to dethrone ourselves from the centre of our world and put another there, and to honour the inviolable sanctity of every single human being, treating everybody, without exception, with absolute justice, equity and respect.

It is also necessary in both public and private life to refrain consistently and empathically from inflicting pain. To act or speak violently out of spite, chauvinism, or self-interest, to impoverish, exploit or deny basic rights to anybody, and to incite hatred by denigrating others—even our enemies—is denial of our common humanity. We acknowledge that we have failed to live compassionately and that some have even increased the sum of human misery in the name of religion.

We therefore call upon all men and women to restore compassion to the centre of morality and religion ~ to return to the ancient principle that any interpretation of scripture that breeds violence, hatred or disdain is illegitimate ~ to ensure that youth are given accurate and respectful information about other traditions, religions and cultures ~ to encourage a positive appreciation of cultural and religious diversity ~ to cultivate an informed empathy with the suffering of all human beings—even those regarded as enemies.

We urgently need to make compassion a clear, luminous and dynamic force in our polarized world. Rooted in a principled determination to transcend selfishness, compassion can break down political, dogmatic, ideological and religious boundaries. Born of our deep interdependence, compassion is essential to human relationships and to a fulfilled humanity. It is the path to enlightenment, and indispensable to the creation of a just economy and a peaceful global community.

Inspired by the original charter, a Children's Charter for Compassion was created by Erin Henry and launched the following year. Henry says the primary goal of the Children's Charter is "to provide a means for children and those around them to understand how to treat themselves and others with love, kindness and ultimately with compassion in simple, easy to understand language. By implementing The Golden Rule, 'do unto others as you will have done to yourself', world peace can be achieved. It begins with our children."

As someone who was involved at the beginnings of the local and global kindness movement, and has now been involved with the compassion movement for a number of years, I know there are countless ordinary people doing extraordinary things under the banner of compassion.

The Charter for Compassion and The Golden Rule offer guidance; the rest is up to us. The requirement is that we practice—and allow others to practice—compassion in our private and public lives. It is okay to wear your heart on your sleeve whether at a worship service, the dinner table, or the corporate boardroom.

It all comes back to having a devotion to being the change we want and need to see in the world.

A Personal Charter

Joseph M. Marshall, author of *The Lakota Way* and a Native American elder, offers this insight for us to consider: "Respect for all forms of life, unfortunately, is not a common value in many cultures today. It is easier to respect someone stronger, faster, or richer. Likewise, it is easy to respect someone who is much like us in every way possible. Respecting someone with different beliefs, different dress, or different customs—or something entirely different from us—is not easy."

From my work in human resources, I have learned that it is our judgments that separate us, not our differences. The food we eat, our age, our country of origin, our gender, income, and street address can take the blame for dividing us. In truth, these differences don't. It is our judgments that create division, that turn trivia into tyranny in our personal encounters.

We need to consciously sort our way through the judgments we habitually make. Ask yourself and others thought-provoking questions and be willing to open the door to stimulating conversation. Learn more about someone else's beliefs or denomination by reading or attending a service. Welcome others to your exploration.

In considering what Joseph Marshall says, would you be able to articulate what you respect, what your values are, and how you live them? If you were to compose your own Charter, what would your core principles be? What Golden Rule would guide you?

A Friend and Companion

A Charter is a collective and comprehensive way of sharing and expressing the principles of compassion. A personal charter as suggested above would express your individualized allegiance. There are also informal and spontaneous ways to explore and capture your thoughts. Charters, poetry, chat, or notes—each of these is a way of setting an intention to live a more compassionate life.

While on a recent business trip, I was unwillingly strapped into my airplane seat with the "do not walk about the cabin" light blinking at me. I gave myself the length of time it would take for the safety belt sign to disengage and release me to record random and uncensored thoughts about this "alive" presence in my life. Here are my original, unaltered scribbles:

> Compassion doesn't care what your suit size is and if you put on a little extra weight
>
> Or whether you can look someone in the eye and show you are confident.
>
> It doesn't care if you have too little or too much money
>
> Or whether you replied to an email promptly or have the latest technology.

> It doesn't care if your family is odd, and different, and little bit crazy
>
> Or if you are odd, and different, and little bit crazy.
>
> It doesn't care if your home looks like a rummage sale and needs dusting
>
> Or what the square footage of your house is and what zip code it belongs to.
>
> It doesn't care if your nails are manicured and your lipstick is on
>
> Or if your hair is grey, curly, straight, or even if you don't have any.
>
> It doesn't care if you have a degree, spell properly, and write clearly
>
> Or even less what color your skin is and what country you live in or your age.
>
> It doesn't care if you have the right words to say at the right time.
>
> Compassion only cares that you step forward and say, "How may I be of service?"

What I noticed was that compassion holds no judgments, believes in my unlimited potential, and always wishes the best for me. It is like a loyal and silent friend who walks beside me regardless of what muddled and messy day I am having.

If you were to do a similar exercise while the kettle comes to a boil, what gifts and insights would compassion offer you?

An Alive Presence

Dale understands the alive presence of compassion—how it lives when we embrace it. Her inspiring free verse poem is titled, "From Deep Within," which she penned regarding her belief about compassion's ability to connect to all that is above, below, around, and within us.

> Music
>
> connects us
>
> to the universe,
>
> Nature
>
> to our soul.
>
> Art,
>
> to our invisible-fragmented parts,
>
> is a mosaic portal
>
> capable of erasing the barriers
>
> to who we are...
>
> to who we can be.
>
> Each work of art,

each courageous completion,

is bonded

by compassion for What Was...

and a New Vision

of What-Is-To-Be.

Find Your Path

How can we bring the alive presence of compassion into our own hearts? I believe we may do so through discovering our personal form of devotion.

Because of its roots in religious worship, "devotion" is a word that has been, for many, divorced from modern life. And yet, I argue fervently that devotion also stands firmly as a lay word. It is a contemplative and self-reflective process. At its core, it is meant to be an inward journey that will ultimately inspire how we express ourselves in the outer world.

For some of us this may show up in following a faith-based path, while others walk a path of devotion to their families and friends. Talk to a pet parent or

> We have committed the golden rule to memory; let us now commit it to life.
>
> Edwin Markham

gardener and you will see devotion in their eyes. Start up a conversation with a social activist and he will share his hope for positive change. Perhaps you know someone who is committed to healthy living, yoga, or running.

On this journey to put compassion into action, we may find our own way by allowing ourselves contemplative time to find our devotion. It is not necessary to go off on a retreat to the emerald green forest. Contemplation can take place while you are getting on with life, making a meal, driving your car, taking the bus, or conversing with a friend. The "where" really does not matter; the key is being open to receiving.

In grade one, I walked home from school one day with my own so-very-precious "golden ruler," which had the saying engraved on the back. I treasured that shiny ruler, as though it were true bullion, for years. Eventually most of the tinted finish wore off. The ruler was no longer polished and glistening, and my child-self lost interest in it, but the implication and importance of the words inscribed on the ruler have never departed far from me. I may not have always lived up to its message and yet, whenever I practice The Golden Rule, I feel my heart blossom and my soul strengthen.

In the same way, allowing compassion to live in our hearts nurtures and guides us in a way that is gentle and true. As Dale alludes, art, nature, and music connect us to the living presence of compassion within us. I will add that writing and conversation may do the same.

Contemplative time allows us to remember what is good and right and meaningful in our lives. It allows us to reset our compass to our true north. Devotion offers us a means to connect to our inner spirit and to express our compassionate selves mindfully in the world.

There is no accurate path for devotion, because it is our path—and ours alone—to discover and explore.

Discern Your Own Devotion

I would like to return to the company of Nancy and her son, Chris. She wrote that her son has been her greatest teacher…

> He is self-sufficient with his activities of daily living, surprising those who said he would "never walk and never talk." He graduated from high school (a year behind) and is now an accomplished song writer. He loves to tell stories and jokes to those who take the time to listen, forever captivating them with his infectious laugh.
>
> I do not know anyone else who has the determination and patience, kindness and compassion that Chris has. I am honored to have the privilege of being his mother. Each time I see another "special one" I take a moment to appreciate

> that each person who is sent to us with a disability has been sent for a reason. My son has taught me invaluable lessons in the practice of unconditional acceptance of self and others, mindfulness and living in the moment, gratitude, and self-determination.
>
> Chris is twenty-seven years old now and plays the slide guitar in a blues band and continues to work on producing an album with his many musician friends...

When we divine what gives our lives purpose and meaning, when we put that understanding into practice, no matter how frail or tentative we may feel ourselves to be, we find our most profound human calling. We find the beating heart that gives life to charters and golden rules, that inspires poetry, deed, and reflection. We find the epicenter that lies at the heart of compassion itself.

A devotion.

Chapter 3

A Science

Science without religion is lame, religion without science is blind.

Albert Einstein

Keep feeling the need for being first. But I want you to be first in love. I want you to be first in moral excellence. I want you to be first in generosity.

Martin Luther King, Jr.

To convert "compassion" to a verb, we look through the lens of science. What do scholars in neuroscience, behavioral science, medicine, and zoology have in common? Despite working in widely differing disciplines, many are being drawn to investigate how compassion plays a vital and living role in their fields of study.

The inclusion of compassion in such studies reflects the stretch and pull at the fabric of science. Centuries ago, scholars delved into alchemy, astrology, and astronomy in their search for knowledge. In the past century, the ascendance of the scientific method focused the study of science on the material world and its laws.

Albert Einstein, one of the greatest scientists in history, perhaps expressed his reservations about that focus and signaled a paradigm shift when he wrote: "A human being is a part of the whole called by us universe, a part limited in time and space. He experiences himself, his thoughts and feelings as something separated from the rest, a kind of optical delusion of his consciousness. This delusion is a kind of prison for us, restricting us to our personal desires and to affection for a few persons nearest to us. Our task must be to free ourselves from this prison by widening our circle of compassion to embrace all living creatures and the whole of nature in its beauty."

The compassion Einstein describes cannot be reduced to test tubes and formulae; but its invisibility does not render it irrelevant or inessential. Instead, I would argue a science of compassion is crucial to our sustained evolution as individuals and members of society. Just as medical science endeavors to bring health and healing to the physical body, so a science of compassion must endeavor to bring health and healing to not just the corporeal body, but the spiritual body of individuals and community.

The man in the blue maintenance uniform inspired me to answer my Koan—my question: *what is compassion?* Inadvertently, he called on me to widen my understanding of, and enquiry into, compassion so I would look at this powerful word from a multitude of angles and disciplines. From my own experience and research, I can attest that the science of compassion is a living, breathing, and exciting field of work, filled with discovery, possibility, and hope.

Measuring the Immeasurable

Science demands measurement and quantifiable objectives. Is it possible to measure compassion? Can it be as easily quantified as a test tube filled with chemicals?

I once observed a gentleman panhandling for money using a very creative approach. At his feet he had two decorated shoeboxes—one in pink labeled "Female Vote" and the other in blue labeled "Male Vote." He was holding a sign that asked, "Which one is the most generous?" I could not help but smile and donate.

After making my contribution to his study, I asked if I could check the results. He let me open the boxes and peek in to do a quick count, but alas, my curiosity remained unsatisfied: I could not declare a winner. Perhaps his unofficial tally offers a working hypothesis: men and women are indistinguishable when we give out of compassion and humor.

Aside from the shoebox system, the World Giving Index undertakes the measuring and ranking of countries based on the charitable actions of their citizens in the past 30 days and what they have done by way of financial donations, volunteering, and helping strangers. Surely these actions reflect compassion in action.

The Index surveys 153 countries using The Gallup Organization. Its findings reveal phenomena I find curious and enlightening: the quantity of giving does not reflect the material wealth accumulated by its citizens, but rather how happy the citizens of a country feel. Perhaps the shoebox man had instinctively grasped this finding. I recollect the small crowd of people gathered about him enjoying the humor of his display.

The shoebox man and the World Giving Index both relied on charitable donations to measure compassion in action. Of course, one can make a donation out of selfish reasons, and surely, when tax receipts are added up, and a quantifiable, provable number is reached, one might argue that there's no compassion in action here—these donations were made to get tax refunds.

The Fraser Institute is an international think tank linked with 85 other think tanks globally, which includes a research roster of 350 authors, six of whom have been given the Nobel Peace Prize. The 2012 Generosity Index is one of their many studies that are released specific to North America to measure citizen donations to "enhance quality of life in their communities and beyond."

The final numbers they use are only what are officially declared on income tax returns. I was curious to find out whether citizens give only because they can write their donations off as a tax deduction. If so, how deeply meaningful and compassionate can that donation actually be?

In *The American,* an online magazine of the American Enterprise Institute, author Arthur C. Brooks spoke to this very topic in 2008: "We are a nation of givers, and in what form does it feed our souls and hearts? Still, tax deductibility is actually irrelevant for most people. IRS records show that only about a third of people who file tax returns itemize their deductions—which means that most Americans don't even claim the deductions to which they are entitled. Furthermore, research shows that virtually no one is motivated meaningfully to give only because of our tax system."

Thus, we can measure the money, but it seems that something without substance, yet truly powerful, plays a deeper role in the giving. It affects the amount measured and yet, it seems, cannot be adequately measured. There are numbers, and they are helpful, educational, and enlightening; but they do not capture the essence of compassion in action.

A University Decree

Universities have been the harbingers, the purveyors, and the seats of radical knowledge and groundbreaking understanding over the centuries. Today, they are world leaders in studying compassion as a science.

Stanford University has established a world-renowned center aptly named the Center for Compassion and Altruism Research and Education (CCARE). Using a multidisciplinary approach, the Center's objective is to conduct research on compassion and altruism. In a roundtable discussion I attended with leading individuals in the field of compassion, Dr. James Doty, Director of CCARE, shared with us his passion for a global compassion movement. Together, he argues, our collective ideas would create undeniable bench strength; individually, he emphasized, we are not as strong as the whole.

CCARE has a definitive goal of researching benevolent acts. At the same time, it is creating user-friendly tools and training to allow individuals to engage in altruistic actions. CCARE is not simply a center for study, it is a locus for compassion in action. Its mandate is not just about gathering

> This virtue, one of the noblest with which man is endowed, seems to arise incidentally from our sympathies becoming more tender and more widely diffused, until they are extended to all sentient beings.
>
> Charles Darwin

quantitative research data, but how to create compassion: how to spread it like a positive contagious virus. CCARE holds conferences and workshops with prominent speakers and, most recently, they have developed a compassion wiki to create a comprehensive dictionary on compassion as well as a database to explore empirical research on compassion and empathy.

Hailing from the University of California, Berkley, the Greater Good Science Center "studies the psychology, sociology, and neuroscience of well-being" and "teaches skills that foster a thriving, resilient, and compassionate society." This significant mission statement guides their research in compassion as well as the six additional themes of gratitude, mindfulness, forgiveness, happiness, empathy, and altruism. Using podcasts, articles, discussion forums, and events they showcase their studies and many other outstanding bodies of research under one roof.

New York's Stony Brook University has founded the Center for Medical Humanities, Compassionate Care, and Bioethics. The Center works with over 40 universities to better understand and teach compassionate care in the medical field. It may seem odd that the medical profession needs to do research on compassionate care, as we make the assumption that this is innate within the field. Having worked for years in healthcare as a consultant, I can testify that those working in the medical field will tell you they need more compassionate care all around—both toward each other and toward patients.

Another stellar institution is The Dalai Lama Center for Peace and Education, founded in 2005 in Vancouver, Canada. The Center has the honor of being one of the few institutions to which His Holiness the Dalai Lama has endorsed the use of his name. My colleague, CEO Lynn Green, tells me their mandate has been to address the Dalai Lama's question, "How can we educate the hearts of children?" The Center works closely with educators, leading scholars, and cognitive neuroscience researchers to explore the competencies of compassion and empathy.

Green says one of their core focuses has been on "social and emotional learning, which has been identified as a core competency to be integrated into kindergarten to grade 12 curriculums and assessment framework." Leading researchers alongside whom the Center works claim we have "the capacity for compassion and empathy; it can be taught and learned in different stages, but optimally, the earlier the better." "Education," adds Green, "is embracing this dimension of children's learning to build skills and empathy for others."

Helper's High

Medical science has discovered ways to alleviate human ailments and suffering. Aspirin, insulin, antidepressants—any number of medications have been scientifically proven to enhance our well-being. Can compassion do the same?

"Helper's high" is a phrase that originated in the late 1980s with Allan Luks, who was the executive director of the global Big Brothers and Big Sisters organization at that time. Luks was curious about the side effects of benevolent actions and proceeded to survey 3,000 adult volunteers. When the results came in, an astounding number—namely 95 percent—had experienced positive feelings after volunteering their services.

Furthering his research in 2001, Luks and co-author Peggy Payne wrote a book called, *The Healing Power of Doing Good—The Health and Spiritual Benefits of Helping Others*. The authors defined "helper's high" as a "euphoric feeling, followed by a long period of calm, experienced after performing a kind act." Their research indicated that individuals who experience "helper's high" routinely report that they experience fewer colds, an increase in joy and self-esteem, less stress, and even less physical pain.

I saw "helper's high" firsthand while at work in India. The Home for the Destitute and Dying is a dismal label for a place where one may reside for the rest of one's life; and yet, there was rarely a moment when this name affected our attitudes. Residents were not made to feel that this was their hopeless fate, but rather, that it was their providence.

For the Missionaries of Charity, the Home, as we called it, was divine intervention. This was a family of blended brothers and sisters with various levels of functionality, not unlike many of our own families, and most importantly, it was their residence of hope, faith, and refuge from the darkness out of which they had walked.

Every resident was also expected to contribute—regardless of their physical, mental, or emotional capacity. The philosophy was: there is always someone in worse condition than you are; therefore, you are responsible to be a brother's or sister's keeper, allowing you the blessing of being of service to someone less fortunate than yourself.

If you have only one hand, you may feed your sister who has no use of her hands. If you can hear and speak, then you become the ears and voice for those who are deaf or have lost their voice. If you can see, then you are the eyes for those who cannot. And if you can walk, then you are the legs of those who are crippled.

Mira, whose radiant smile lit up any room long after she had left, was always busy doing something for someone. The only wheelchair on the premises was designated for Mira because she had been born without any legs, and sadly, had been abandoned on the streets of New Delhi as an infant. While her left arm was a stump up to her elbow, she did have the full use of her right hand. Mira spent her days knitting colorful scarves and hats for the women to wear during the crisp winter months.

Each day I continued to be astonished at her capacity to weave those brightly dyed wools at record speed. My two good hands had never mastered learning to knit and I had given it up impatiently, never finishing anything that I had started. Mira reminded me, without saying a word, that I had given up too easily. In Mira's sunniness and contribution, I saw how helper's high was as vital a life force as the warmth of security the home had to offer.

An Aspirin a Day

It is common knowledge that an aspirin a day not only clears up any headaches, but promotes heart health and may prevent strokes. Can acts of compassion also be good for our heart?

Dr. Myriam Mongrain of York University in Toronto, Canada, has been conducting studies to ascertain whether there is indeed an enduring effect after a good deed is done. She monitored a test group of over 700 subjects who, for one week, were asked to do something nice for someone each day in some small way, even for as little as 15 minutes. After a week of good deeds the subjects were asked to stop and were interviewed six months later to see whether there were any lasting effects on the lives of the participants.

The result concluded that over 50 percent of participants voluntarily continued doing good deeds—even after they could have stopped—because they felt an improved sense of well-being. Some participants even stated that the experiment had actually changed their lives for the better. Mongrain concluded, "What's amazing is that the time investment required for these changes to occur is so small; we're talking mere minutes a day."

Study subjects also showed an increase in their happiness. Dr. Mongrain's further comments make an interesting allusion to our consideration of compassion as a devotion. "Empathy," she added, "needs to be practiced."

In 2007 a study at Syracuse University noted that people with giving personalities were 42 percent more likely than non-givers to declare they were "very happy" and 25 percent more likely to report they were "in excellent health."

It appears that, like an aspirin per day, acts of compassion promote a sense of well-being. Can acts of compassion also help us live longer?

At the University of Michigan, Dr. Marc A. Musick and his researchers interviewed and collected data from 2,011 older adults for 7.5 years. It was found that, even if the seniors spent less than an hour a week volunteering, these moderate levels of volunteering increased their chances of survival.

The benefits of volunteering have been surprising researchers since 1956. That year, a study was commenced at Cornell University to find out whether a typical housewife of the time, with more children than average, would live under greater stress and therefore experience an earlier death. The researchers followed the lives of 427 married women with children for a period of 30 years.

When they compiled the results, what they discovered astonished them.

The number of children had no effect on the longevity of the subject. Nor did the economic class, type of work, or level of education. What came next was the surprise discovery. The researchers also looked into whether or not the women in their study also volunteered. Among

> Give, Receive, Dance! When you begin to touch your heart or let your heart be touched, you begin to discover that it's bottomless.
>
> Pema Chodron

those who did not volunteer, 52 percent experienced a major illness. Among those who did volunteer, 36 percent experienced a major illness—a startling decrease of 16 percent.

How wonderful to discover that a few minutes of daily practice create an increase in happiness and sense of well-being while affecting the life of someone else in a positive way. How astonishing to think that it may also play a role in making one's life not just happier, but longer.

That's one powerful aspirin per day.

Therapeutic Helper's High

Over time, "helper's high" has become a therapeutic technique referred to as "helper therapy." Dr. Frank Riessman, a social psychologist, first brought this model to light in 1965 by observing a self-help group, namely Alcoholics Anonymous, and discovered that the act of supporting another person with the same condition as you actually supports the helper to heal—more so than the receiver—supporting the theory of reciprocity.

A wise saying suggests that we walk in another person's shoes to understand him. Perhaps an even wiser saying would suggest that, if we have worn those tattered shoes and danced in them ourselves, we have even more to offer those we seek to help. How can one not have more natural empathy and an intimate connection when you have been there, done that, and bought the T-shirt yourself?

Ralph Waldo Emerson once wrote: "It is one of the most beautiful compensations of life that no man can sincerely try to help another without helping himself." This method of helper therapy has been tried and proven in treating everything from addiction, weight loss, grief, depression, and pain. It also plays an active role in business and professional associations where colleagues mentor others in the same field.

The Compassionate Brain

We know that exercise makes us healthy and creates physiological benefits. Can acts of compassion do the same?

Emory University, a leading private research university in Atlanta, Georgia, whose mission is to "create, preserve, teach and apply knowledge in the service of humanity," has studied activity in the brain using a functional magnetic resonance imaging (fMRI) scanner after subjects played a game based on reciprocal altruism. Apparently, our brains receive much more blood oxygen flow while undertaking altruistic actions, and essentially lights up with a glow. Also, what was notable was that the same areas of the brain beam as when a person is the recipient of a reward or is having a pleasurable experience. Altruism, it appears, can be a real turn-on.

In the world of science and substantive data, it is encouraging to discover the Institute for Research on Unlimited Love. Based in Ohio, this non-profit was established with support from philanthropist John Templeton and the Templeton Foundation, with a clear mandate to support high levels of empirical research involving distinguished academia on topics related to unselfish love, compassion, altruism, and service and its origins.

Dr. Stephen Post, from Stony Brook University, is also the Executive Director of the Institute and writes extensively on their stellar research into the brain and compassion. Quoting Dr. Post, he tells us there is a "care-and-connection" part of our brains that allows us to experience extreme states of joy when we give to others. He says, "It doesn't come from any dry action—where the act is out of duty in the narrowest sense, like writing a check for a good cause. It comes from working to cultivate a generous quality—from interacting with people. There is the smile, the tone in the voice, the touch on the shoulder. We're talking about altruistic love."

MRI scans of the brain are revealing that specific brain regions become activated when we experience compassionate emotions. Many centuries ago, Thomas Aquinas, the Italian

Dominican Roman Catholic priest known as one of the world's great theologians and philosophers, said, "I would rather feel compassion than know the meaning of it."

Without an MRI to support him, he revealed the true secret of compassion in action—when one commits a benevolent act, one feels it profoundly. Studying the brain and our physiology when we behave compassionately only substantiates what we have long known: doing good deeds in the world is good for us.

The Spark Plug

You can jump out of an airplane with a parachute, but unless you open it, what good will it do? You may have a deep yearning to do good in the world, but unless you act upon it, what good will you do? Can science help you jumpstart the innate generous self you have lurking within? Your brain chemicals can indeed be activated so you may engage in and live a more generous life.

A little hormone named oxytocin acts as a neurotransmitter in the brain and is largely involved in our social and emotional processes. This worker bee is responsible for many of our chief emotional responses; its presence increases our sense of compassion, empathy, sacrifice, and even forgiveness. It plays a role in maternal bonding and romance;

it increases trust and decreases fear. I think we should rename it the CEO of neurotransmitters because of its intense job description and the array of emotions it manages.

This hormone is also action oriented. My own experience and reading have suggested to me that many of the intangible aspects of compassionate acts are actually now tangible and can be quantified and qualified by scientific study. Dr. Paul J. Zak, Professor of Economics, Psychology, and Management, and founding Director of the Center for Neuroeconomics Studies at Claremont Graduate University, as well as author of *The Moral Molecule,* has done groundbreaking work on how oxytocin affects and benefits us.

Dr. Zak's studies reveal what I would call an essential link in our evolution: they demonstrate that raising oxytocin levels also raises one's level of generosity and compassion. One of Zak's landmark studies gave test subjects 10 dollars and asked them to give away a percentage of it to total strangers. Subjects given a dose of synthetic oxytocin through a nasal spray were an astounding 80 percent more generous than those who did not receive the spray.

The notion of being able to boost our generosity quotient is both tangible and gratifying. The road to compassion is a joyful one; the steps are simple and the way doesn't have to be complex or difficult if we listen to the cues that science is offering up to help ourselves increase our oxytocin levels for our own well-being and for distribution to others through the delivery of more generous acts.

There are multiple entry points to boosting oxytocin in our brains without the use of a nasal spray. Dr. Zak's research indicates the brain naturally produces oxytocin during prayer, meditation, and in the delivery of warm, affectionate actions such as hugs or holding hands. The recall of a wonderful memory in detail; dancing closely with a special partner; and enjoying a massage treatment also stimulate the release of oxytocin.

Step one in jumpstarting your compassionate self is to be more affectionate. Through the effortless act of hugging someone you will boost the chemical oxytocin into gear—allowing the floodgates to open and inundate your entire system. As your hormone levels elevate, a sense of well-being will kick in as fast as eating your favorite comfort food, and with a lot fewer calories.

Dr. Zak and his team of researchers have also studied intimate relationships and the role of oxytocin. In order for an individual to nurture a healthy romantic connection, he or she only needs to hug for twenty seconds. Oxytocin will spike because there is already an established relationship and memory. Along with this spike there will be increased benefits: a decrease in heart rate, blood pressure, and the stress hormone, cortisol.

Hugging a loved one for 20 seconds is an enjoyable prescription to fill. You may even want to venture out farther and hug a neighbor or a colleague today and start a positive chain reaction of oxytocin in your surrounding environment.

Step two in jumpstarting your compassionate self is to enjoy a contemplative practice such as prayer, meditation, or time in nature. It is being conscious of seeking out calming self-care time that is nurturing to the body and spirit. This reflective personal time grants an opportunity to recharge and center oneself from the constant barrage of chaos that can slowly eat away at our oxytocin reserve.

I muse on how the world might look if we could shake a little oxytocin on our eggs in the morning—like salt and pepper—and begin our day with a different perspective. And yet, we don't need to. Oxytocin is there, waiting to be released; it's like a spark plug for igniting us with inspiration so we may act with altruism and compassion.

Compassion is Good Medicine

Recently, I was the keynote speaker for a nationwide long-term care provider where the CEO opened the conference with a powerful comment regarding the presence of affection and the need for the warmth human contact brings. He said, "We have plenty of handling of our residents, but I am not so sure they get as much touch." He then urged his leadership team to ensure that "touch" was what their business was all about.

Dr. Zak's research corroborates this assertion. He recommends people give and receive a minimum of eight hugs per day in order to stay connected to others and to feel a greater sense of happiness.

And yet, some technological advancement in science is pushing against these discoveries. One such example is the invention of robotic care providers replacing human caregivers. Japanese researchers have recently created a "soft" robot that has the capability to pick up and move the weight of an adult body. The original concept was to fill a pending skills and labor shortage for their rapidly aging population with the long-range intention of these robots being used in the average household.

Thus far, sales have been limited. I am sure it is in large part because people recoil from the notion of being picked up by mechanical arms. Given the choice, they choose the warmth of human contact. We know instinctively that human touch is crucial to our well-being, yet we still play with the idea of removing the human element from many arenas of customer service. I somehow doubt that a robot, regardless of how "soft" this androgynous immortal is, has the capability of sharing a sense of caring and connectedness—and certainly not compassion.

Compassion Creates Good Memories

Sudan wrote to me about an experience she had while working as a volunteer for her Rotary Club and the Bill & Melinda Gates Foundation to collect loose change. The long-term goal of the project is to eradicate polio worldwide.

> We gave out balloons to all the kids that came by and wrote their names or personalized messages on them. I saw two little kids walking by with their parents and they were both crying, tears just streaming down their faces. So I walked out of my booth and asked them if they wanted a balloon. They all came over and we blew up some balloons and wrote their names on them.
>
> All of a sudden, the tears stopped and they were both smiling and happy just holding these balloons. Their mom smiled and thanked me and told me I had saved the day. So not only did we raise money to end polio for kids around the world but also put a smile on the faces of two beautiful kids right here.

Science could study everyone involved and show how their physiologies changed over the course of the scene, but we instinctively know the results. Sudan's compassionate gesture wiped away the children's tears and replaced them with smiles. Her simple act changed the parents' frustration to pleasure. A bond was created between parents and child and stranger, and everyone's frame of mind was changed.

Sudan still remembers that day—it is quite possible that the parents and children will always remember it as well. She uplifted everyone and the memory of that moment can live on and create good will and compassion for so long as it is cultivated.

If I were to offer a third step to jumpstarting your compassionate self, it would be to practice recalling happy memories.

The Compassion of Animals

We read the stories and see them on YouTube, and our hearts and minds are opened by the bonding and compassion that exists in the animal world. A dog and elephant are friends, a mother cat adopts a rabbit, dolphins assist pygmy whales in distress, and elephants mourn their dead.

Frans de Waal studies animal behavior and has found acts of consolation, reconciliation, and cooperation among chimpanzees and apes. His work and theories have inspired opposing theories about the meaning of these interactions, but to me, there is something simple at work—compassion. It is innate and natural.

English naturalist Charles Darwin is identified with Herbert Spencer's phrase "survival of the fittest," which was used in his 1871 book, *The Descent of Man*. Society has used this as a banner for maintaining that competition is healthy and normal, and that the weaker are not worthy of survival.

And yet, when a content analysis was taken of his book, the phrase "survival of the fittest" only appears twice; selfishness makes 12 appearances, and competition is counted 9 times. Love, however, appears 95 times, mutuality 24 times, and moral sensitivity 92 times.

A Tree Full of Apples

Our mothers used to tell us to eat an apple a day, and quite often we could pick one from a tree in the neighborhood. Compassion is like that. It is a tree full of bounty and good medicine. And, like a tree, it offers beauty and sustenance so that all who take shelter under its canopy may thrive.

When it comes to sustaining healthy individuals and communities, compassion is good medicine. Good science merely shows us what we innately know.

Chapter 4

Compassionate Optimism

Somewhere, something incredible is waiting to be known.

Carl Sagan

We do not see things as they are. We see things as we are.

Anais Nin

Compassionate optimism—we do not usually associate these two words with each other, let alone conjoined as though they belong together.

Our traditional understanding of compassion draws us to words laden with pain and suffering, while optimism uplifts us with positive thoughts, hopefulness, and cheer. Put these two contrasting words together and they are as much an oxymoron as "jumbo shrimp," "auto pilot," or even, "working lunch."

And yet, when compassion and optimism combine, they become a powerful expression of language: each word supports and lifts up the other to higher ground, much like two good friends.

And, like good friends, these words cannot offer a panacea to fix what may not be fixable in one's life. But what they can offer is a graceful opportunity to reframe our experience in terms that offer us strength and hope and, yes…optimism!

You know you are acquainted with an optimist when you share that life had just handed you a sour lemon and they listen, and, while you talk with them, they help you discover you have sugar, water, and everything possible to create a glass of sweet lemonade. It may not be easy or simple, but you feel that possibility. And you know you are conversing with a pessimist when you share the same news and they ask you to pass the tequila and salt in order to wallow with you in misery and stay there.

In their own ways, perhaps both the optimist and the pessimist are compassionate, and yet only one of them is offering you an option that will ultimately sustain you.

In "A Devotion," Nancy and her son Chris represent compassionate optimists at their best. Their life circumstances are what they are and there is no changing them—and yet, both Nancy and Chris move forward with determination and joyful hearts. They have developed a beautiful inner accord that has supported them and touched countless others who have crossed their path. For both Nancy and Chris, the metaphoric cup is half full, not dismally half empty.

Make Someone Happy

To fully value the power compassionate optimism can play in our lives, it is helpful to know people such as Nancy and Chris who embody its qualities.

Teena volunteers at a rural hospital and wrote to me about her responsibility at the reception desk of day surgery. Patients begin arriving at 6:30 a.m., anxious and nervous about their procedures—their stress, no doubt, heightened because, on ordinary days, optimism may not normally kick in until after they have had several coffees or their lunch.

> Since I love flowers, I started bringing fresh garden-picked flowers in a vase for my desk. To my huge surprise I discovered this to be a conversation starter.
>
> Yes, flowers speak to people.
>
> So, instead of worrying about their surgery or pains, patients were busy discussing the various types and colors of my desk flowers. Especially the elderly patients who would begin to relate how they grew such-and-such, what type of soil worked best, which variety likes sun or shade, or how long the seed has been in the family, some of which came from their grandmothers.
>
> In short, those flowers, which only took a few extra moments to whip in the car, were the star of the morning. Oh, yes, even hurried doctors passing by commented favorably—a happy feeling.
>
> My latest attraction—now that garden flowers are dwindling down—are those perky, bright red cranberries. I

> pick low bush cranberries, which go into a little vase, and now the conversations go into recipes and patients tell me of favorite cranberry muffins, loaves, jellies, or cranberry sauce for Thanksgiving turkey.
>
> This is such a feel-good way of sharing. Is this in my job description? No. Is it in my make-someone-happy description? Yes.

An optimist would bring flowers to brighten a room or make a cheery comment. Teena's motive goes deeper. She and her flowers alleviate, even if only for a short time, the anxiety and distress she observes in those coming in for day surgery. She is an infectious example of how someone acting with compassion and optimism serves hope and care on a platter to whomever she meets.

Teena acquainted me with her personal motto: "When I see someone without a smile I just give them one of mine." I'll take two generous helpings of that dictum any day.

A Dichotomy

The role the compassionate optimist plays is a crucial one because we live in a world of dichotomies, a world that can be cold and cruel as well as warm and welcoming.

"It was the best of times, it was the worst of times,..." Charles Dickens penned this classic opening line in *A Tale of Two Cities,* one of the most famous pieces of literature in history. In their struggle between hope and doubt, optimism and pessimism, Dickens's characters reflect how we ourselves struggle with the same seesaws and swings in our views and fortunes. The opening continues:

> ...it was the age of wisdom, it was the age of foolishness, it was the epoch of belief, it was the epoch of incredulity, it was the season of Light, it was the season of Darkness, it was the spring of hope, it was the winter of despair, we had everything before us, we had nothing before us, we were all going direct to Heaven, we were all going direct the other way...

For me, these words very much mirror the life I have lived. I am not convinced that there is anyone among us who is entirely an optimist or pessimist. We all balance on the tightrope dividing these two diametrically opposed states of being. In our daily lives, in the situations we encounter, we do the best we can with what we have to work with at the time.

Dichotomy is a form of separation—or, more accurately, the perception of separation, which occurs naturally in the universe around us. Trees and plants live with separation every time one branch splits off and proceeds to create a new branch so the cycle of life can continue.

In the world of astronomy dichotomy is present when the moon or a planet has half of its surface showing as the sun illuminates it with light—while at the same time the other half of the surface remains in darkness. The entire planet is still there; the planet has not gone anywhere, except it has the appearance of being absent.

Just as the planets have two surfaces, so do we—lightness and darkness—which are both present under the surface of who we are. Every one of us would dream of an optimistic and joyful life; yet, who among us has not been weary and exhausted by the stress of modern life?

The dichotomy is that we may choose compassionate optimism or pessimism. Kathleen's approach is one of optimism as she offered her comments on how important the moment of choice is for us.

> Compassion to me is always trying to the thing that assists the moment forward in the best possible way, like forwarding kindness even when I really might not have a totally compassionate mind-set in that moment. But practicing compassion changes that moment and I always hope it might change a small fraction of another person's life experience so that they too can forward compassion to another, hoping it becomes contagious.

What a splendid reminder that we have a responsibility to "assist the moment forward in the best possible way."

If we were to keep her statement front and center as a mantra, it could make a difference in how we enter into messy circumstances—allowing us to come out the other side much differently.

Learning Optimism

Whether optimism springs from nature or nurture is a source of debate among researchers.

We have all met someone who has been blessed by nature with a cheery and optimistic outlook. I have often wondered what combination of genes or chemistry concocts that cheery disposition and whether or not it is nature or nurture.

But there is hope for those who are not naturally blessed with an optimistic approach. Researchers do agree that environmental factors may nurture optimism. I would argue that we may be capable of acquiring optimism as adults and that, like the spreading of a positive virus, we may even be able to infect others with optimism.

> The average pencil is seven inches long, with just a half-inch eraser—in case you thought optimism was dead.
>
> Robert Brault

Dr. Martin Seligman is a well-respected psychologist whose work on "learned helplessness" and "learned optimism" was groundbreaking. His studies found that feelings of helplessness could actually be induced in subjects—that, through their experience of recurring negative events, subjects actually adopted an expectation of failure, and as a result, were unlikely to take action to change the outcome of a given situation. They had, in effect, learned to be helpless. Dr. Seligman's team observed that some subjects would never become helpless while others would gravitate toward it with more ease.

After further study, Dr. Seligman's team of researchers shifted their focus. If helplessness and pessimism were learned behaviors, could it be possible to unlearn them? Could it be possible to learn optimism?

The theory of Positive Psychology was born. We should not focus solely on our ailments, but also on how to thrive, be resilient, and be happy. We can learn optimism, and this learning will affect our resilience and expectations when we are confronted with problems to solve. As optimists, we are more motivated to find a solution; as pessimists, we are more inclined to give up on, or avoid, an issue.

Learning that one can actually create an optimistic state of mind as well as build new competencies is groundbreaking and exciting for individuals wanting to shift their present state from passive to active.

In one study, researchers selected a group of first-year university students they determined to be prone to pessimism. Half of the group became the control group—the students did not change any of their behavior patterns. The remaining students attended a 16-hour workshop, during which they were given instruction and techniques on how to be more optimistic.

The research team followed up 18 months later. They discovered that 32 percent of the control group had undergone moderate to severe depression and 15 percent had experienced moderate to severe anxiety. Of the group that had attended the training program, 22 percent reported depression and 7 percent suffered anxiety issues. The same group also reported fewer health problems. With a mere 16 hours spent on learning how to think and act differently, substantial change was possible.

Solving a Mystery

Many believe there is a mystery—perhaps an inescapable, unassailable force—underlying why some of us have a propensity for optimism or pessimism. Science may offer us an insight here, a gauge by which we can actually measure this propensity and answer the question: does it govern us? Are we 100 percent under its sway?

A growing body of research indicates that we do indeed have a natural "resting place" we inherit—a state of being that is governed by the traits and characteristics our families have passed on over generations. It is thought that this innate barometer may affect our penchant toward optimism or pessimism by as much as 50 percent.

What, then, of the remaining 50 percent?

A remarkable 40 percent is under our control. Studies from renowned researchers such as Dr. Sonja Lyubomirsky indicate that this astounding 40 percent is our capacity to make deliberate and intentional actions—to be intentionally optimistic or pessimistic. We each have a 40 percent opening to choose how that moment or experience will be. Not much separates the mystery from our ability to form intent because we are more empowered than we realized. Our energy flows where our intention goes.

And what of the remaining 10 percent?

It's life: the curveballs and unforeseen circumstances thrown our way—the havoc sometimes wreaked on our best-laid plans.

It is encouraging, and most enlightening, to know we all hold within our grasp a 40 percent capacity to change our way of showing up in the world. No matter what your resting state, becoming a compassionate optimist is likely within your grasp.

That is, of course, if we are ready and willing to modify our thinking and actions. The older we are, the more entrenched we may become in our own values and ideals. But that shouldn't stop us. After all, being older may make us a little more stuck—it does not mean we cannot unglue ourselves.

So, don't let your "resting state" interrupt or stall you. Rennie shares this humorous story about her mother who, I think, uses the 40 percent at her disposal to live life to the fullest. Rennie's mother is now in her early 80s.

> One evening a few years ago, when talking on the phone with my mother, I happened to ask her what she had for dinner. When she replied that she had eaten porridge for dinner, I said, "Oh, Mum! Really? Porridge?"
>
> Detecting my concern, she said, "Don't worry, dear, I had Bailey's on it!"
>
> My mother's ability to take a basic breakfast staple and embellish it with Irish Cream liqueur is typical of her "glass half full" optimistic attitude toward life. That capacity hasn't changed—in fact it has grown—as she has aged. Through numerous injuries and health and other life challenges she has picked herself up, dusted herself off, and faced those challenges with immense compassion for and belief in what she could overcome.

> At age 79, she broke her pelvis and many people were concerned that she wouldn't walk again. She not only returned to her volunteer and community activities, she "held court" from her hospital bed selling tickets for a community fundraising event!

Sadly, I have seen people train-wreck their lives and businesses because of an unwillingness to consciously use the 40 percent at their disposal and let go of what no longer serves them.

There is no doubt that change can be difficult. Amusingly, we have an expectation that everyone around us should change. We clearly see the changes *they* need to make. We may also clearly see the changes *we* need to make, but we are convinced that our changes are much more difficult than anyone else's.

If it is so difficult for us, why are we so hard on others?

Unlearning Old Habits

In a landmark study by Johns Hopkins Hospital, it was found that most patients who had coronary artery bypass surgery knew that they had to change their lifestyle or the disease would be back with a high probability of death. Yet, even with this knowledge, the vast majority was not willing to alter the behaviors that had led to their condition.

Change is not difficult because we are unable to change; change is difficult because we choose not to change. The unlearning of old habits and the relearning of new ones can be crucial to survival.

I like to tell this story to workshop participants. It captures our ability to choose a more optimistic approach and shows the high cost of choosing not to.

The Ogre in the Hills

A young Egyptian boy named Amon is travelling and comes across a small village located deep in an arid valley. As he spends time in the village, he becomes aware that its citizens act as though there is a constant gray cloud hanging over their small community—it seems to be causing the villagers to complain and moan about everything.

There are no fires ablaze for cooking, the animals are neglected and thirsty, even the children and parents look bedraggled. Amon can see the meager crops are weedy—there is barely enough to feed the villagers and not a portion to spare.

Amon is perplexed. He asks the people why they seem so cheerless and don't care about their lands.

"There is a giant ogre that lives on the very top of our highest mountain and he will come whenever he wants and eat us all," they say in unison and groan.

"An ogre, here in this valley? That is not possible," Amon retorts.

"Look up and you will see his face. It is like an alligator and his body is that of a tiger and he spews out a poisonous breath like a serpent."

In disbelief, the boy looks up toward the mountain and beholds the exact monster as they had described him. Amon is brave and says to the villagers, "Don't be afraid. I will climb the mountain and slay the beast that frightens you."

The villagers beg Amon not to go because they know he would surely die at the hands of the ogre.

Against their wishes, Amon starts up the mountain; and although he is afraid, he keeps climbing. The closer he gets to the top, the smaller the ogre seems.

How can that be? When I stayed in the village, the monster was frightening and huge, but as I climb higher up the mountain he becomes smaller.

After hiking all day and night Amon finally reaches the entrance to the ogre's cave. To his amazement the giant is nothing more than a gentle little troll, no larger than a cat.

The troll seems harmless, so he scoops it up, places it gently into his coat pocket, and walks back down the mountain to the village. As the villagers see him walking toward them, they are excited he is alive.

Eagerly, Amon pulls the little troll out of his pocket and explains how he had brought the giant ogre back down the mountain to show them there is nothing to be afraid of.

The villagers are taken aback and ask the troll what his name is. "I go by many names," he says. "Some call me War, some call me Hunger, some call me Death, some call me Disease, and some call me What Might Happen."

I use this story to illustrate how much personal power we surrender emotionally, mentally, and physically when we are willing to endure waiting for the "what might happen" in our lives.

Sometimes we even choose not to make vital changes because we are so afraid of this "what might happen."

In the field of positive psychology, there is a general consensus that happy individuals observe and construe their surroundings in ways that strengthen and reinforce their optimism. They have a propensity to be more positive and hopeful in how they interact with their environment and adapt more readily to what comes their way.

Those who are pessimists see their surroundings in the same way they interpret their world. Their view of events reinforces their pessimism and vice versa. Like the Egyptian villagers, they tilt toward a negative outlook of life and, by their attitudes and actions, may create the very outcomes they fear.

Each of us resides with the ghosts of the unknown surrounding us. The question to explore is how much awareness do we have of these ghosts and personal "ogres." Are we willing to climb up the mountain and face them? We so often forget that the looming terrible giant stopping us diminishes when we take action.

Becoming a compassionate optimist takes courage and a willingness to examine the choices we have made and want to make. It means taking that 40 percent and starting up the mountain. It means seeing the ogre diminish as it loses its hold on us and our 40 percent increases to 100 percent.

Peaks and Valleys

Compassion coupled with optimism must be grounded in reality. A compassionate optimist does no good wearing Pollyanna glasses in shades of pink and offering bountiful hope that is feeble and lacks substance. Optimism offers no aid when it comes in the form of rose-pigmented icing spread over a cake of pain and suffering, so that we avoid and ignore the truth and the sadness of another.

Tammy, a business consultant, had an idyllic life until the day she was faced with the breakup of her marriage. The permanence and predictability of her life rapidly shifted beneath her feet.

> It seems that when our heart is broken open—and we are feeling a little raw and exposed—that we are also closer to others, we feel more connected and less closed, and we are moved by other people's difficulties. Our hard shell becomes more porous and we can feel and connect easier. This has been my experience in the last five years since being separated and divorced. I used to live in "happy land" and the world I live in now is more real, more fertile and alive, and also more uncomfortable and challenging. Compassion and gratitude are related and expanded when we are in the valleys of our life, not on the top of the mountain.

Another contributor, Paula, wrote that, for her, compassion means being vulnerable "in your heart to the feeling and life situations of another. To see clearly, the individual behind the adversity and move forward in unison, often in a direction that knowingly is uncertain or unknown."

Hardship and change can harden us or make our understanding of life deeper and richer. Both Tammy and Paula offer insight—in order for compassion to be all it can be, it requires empathy and understanding; therefore, we need to be able to recall both the peaks and the heartrending valleys of our life. If we do so, our feelings can be captured, remembered, and then made readily available to access when they are required to assist another.

Simple Joys

Optimism comes from the word "optimize," which is to "make the best of" the circumstances or situation given at that moment. After all, we only have that particular moment in front of us to deal with at any given time. Tammy further wrote that she has also experienced a "greater connection to nature and more awe of what it means to be on the planet and to be human."

Her remarks suggest that we need to optimize where we are now, no matter where that "now" is. If we are lost in this valley of life, making the best of the current situation may be the only way out. This is where a level of hopefulness is essential to our steadfast endurance and where the combination of compassion and optimism for self and others is indispensable to see us through dark periods to light.

As a retired nurse educator and full-time caregiver for her husband, Diane was fully aware that death could come at any time.

> "Diane! Are you there?"
>
> In what I'd deftly dubbed Ingram's Infirmary Inc., I bolted upright from my cot positioned next to my husband's hospital bed in our front room.
>
> Nursing had taught me long ago that humor takes second billing only to hope in dealing with the ill or disabled.

Now, in ministering to my spouse, it had been an invaluable ally once again.

"Yes, Roy, I'm right here, my dear."

"You're looking beautiful this morning," he murmured with a smile.

Roy employed wit to my benefit also: caring for him around the clock following his massive stroke, and now well into our third year of this final odyssey, rendered me many things—but beautiful certainly did not make the mix. It was my cue to chuckle! However often this scene was re-enacted, the charming absurdity of it always brought a grin.

Today, I willed my smile to linger as I rapidly processed the assessment I was accustomed to making. Daunting observations they were, too: each, an ominous omen.

"And how are you feeling this fine morning, Sir?"

"Diane, I don't feel that good. I've got a little trouble getting my breath. Maybe we should go to the hospital."

"We'll see. But, since you're already in Ingram's Infirmary, let's try raising the head of your bed and getting a little oxygen. I think that's all you need. I'll call the palliative care service, and then I'll be right back, okay?"

"Sounds good," he whispered.

I left a message with the receptionist, stressing the severity of my husband's symptoms. An eternity seemed to elapse before a nurse returned my call. I shared my evaluation with her: each unmistakable indicator that confirmed Roy's weakening heart was finally failing fast, his lungs filling with fluid as a result.

"I need oxygen here, right now!"

"Well, all right; but it'll take three hours," she said.

Returning to Roy, I smiled and confirmed, "Oxygen's on the way, my love."

"Oh, that's good," he replied in a weak voice. "When do you think it'll get here?"

Glancing at the clock revealed to both of us that it was 12:20. "It should be here by 1:00."

"That's fine. You know, I feel better already."

Perched on the side of his bed, I took Roy's hands in mine and began to reminisce. Smiling at him, I was rewarded with a weak grin. And, there it was! That twinkle in his eyes that I'd loved for decades flashed by once again.

"And the animals, Roy; think of all the animals. We're in good company right now with our Siamese pair curled up beside you. We've had a number of dogs, Roy, but Siberian huskies are a breed apart. And obviously, a part of you is exactly what Teeka considers herself to be; another constant companion of our days. Remember the scores of orphaned squirrels and five raccoons we fostered? The birds we've befriended, beginning way back with wee Broken Wing? Ah, what adventures we've had with those of the furred and feathered kind!"

As I spoke, I gazed upon a nature mural Roy and I had applied long ago to one wall in this room. In the sky portion of the mural I'd hung a striking sculpture of Canada geese in flight. For me, now, it held a more compelling message. Canada geese, the story goes, mate for life and remain together if one is injured.

Whenever the demands of our situation caused my energy to ebb, I had only to look up at those birds to remind myself that surely I could do as well as a goose.

Suddenly, my monologue was interrupted by a cardinal's whistling call. Though his eyes remained closed now, I saw a gentle smile play across Roy's face. "You hear that, Roy? Our cardinal daddy's come to call."

Glancing out the window revealed fresh pleasures. "And, there's his mate. They delight in the berries dripping

> from the bushes you planted, Roy! Oh, my goodness, they've brought the kids: two pint-sized carbon copies of themselves learning the location of the choicest fare. What a fine little family! And, wait, there's Pee Wee, your beloved squirrel matriarch of seven years, skittering up the maple. We've always known her among all the others, haven't we? They've each dropped by to say hello!"
>
> Pausing briefly, I checked the time: 12:30. "Roy?"
>
> He didn't respond. He didn't need to. Peace rested upon his face like a benediction. I knew he was in "a better place." His long years of suffering, borne without complaint, were over.
>
> We'd succeeded in our effort to complete our earthly journey as a couple where much of it had been lived: at home. The years of caring, while exhausting, were also among the most rewarding of our life together.

Diana shows us how meaningful and compelling compassionate optimism is for bringing light into a room that many would think only holds darkness. The wisdom of compassionate optimism does not mean we ignore our pain or that of others; rather, we acknowledge that we have walked through the shadows of life and felt its sorrows, and yet still savor its simple joys.

Don't Force the Fix or Avoid the Potholes

I do not believe compassionate optimism is about covering up emotions that need to desperately surface—or "fixing" anything for anyone, including oneself. I am of the mind that we spend far too much energy and force trying to "fix" what is supposedly broken within us rather than acknowledging the experience, finding the gifts within it, and moving forward.

However, we have become a culture of addictions, and the drama of personal pain is one of them. The question remains for how long one wants to sit in the muck before moving onward.

I, as well as many readers, will frankly admit that we do not grow and learn when we are coasting along the safe shoreline in our perfect sailboat, with a perfect wind moving us perfectly along in a world devoid of the rocks and whirlpools that sink vessels. Indeed, like others, I relish these calm times when they are with me.

I also no longer endeavor to fight or avoid challenges that come my way, because therein lies the climb to a higher altitude on the mountain. I am getting closer to the ogre, as it were. Or, as a friend once advised me during a particularly uneven time in my life, "Olivia, when you're going through hell, just keep going."

My personal compass to navigate when the waves are rough or the shoreline stony is, "Just breathe; just keep breathing and this will pass." Interestingly, it always does pass. I suspect Ralph Waldo Emerson must have been an optimist, for he once said, "I have had one thousand catastrophes in my life and one or two actually happened."

Taking a more optimistic approach to life is not avoiding the rough spots—for the reason that, try as we might, we all hit potholes in the road no matter how much we try to swerve around them. We may not be able to control our circumstances—an outcome may be out of our hands—but we all have more choices than we realize. We can always most certainly guide and be mindful of our emotional responses. We can cultivate compassionate optimism instead of lapsing into habitual reactions.

Hire for Optimism and Display Compassion

Life does not stop when we come to work; in fact, many occupations can escalate the difficulty of personal circumstances because of the stress they add to one's life. A compassionate approach to people management, therefore, is crucial.

As someone who has spent her livelihood in organizations, by way of my leadership consulting background, I have been actively engaged in recruitment and retention strategies my entire career. I am always on the hunt for new ways to enhance employee engagement and so I look through the lens of compassionate optimism to bring new knowledge to the workplace setting.

Once again, through a groundbreaking study, Dr. Seligman and his team bring to light the central role optimism can play in hiring and work performance.

Traditionally, skills and experience ensured that a candidate's resume rose to the top. In the past decade, there has been more emphasis on hiring for attitude. In this study, hiring based on attitude was taken one step further. A large insurance company agreed to hire candidates with high scores for optimism, even though they may have been less skilled in the role itself.

After two years, Dr. Seligman's team tabulated the results and they were dramatic.

The new employees who had been hired based on their score for optimism were markedly outperforming their counterparts who were more experienced, but also rated as more pessimistic.

Those with more optimistic outlooks outsold the more skilled pessimists by an astounding 57 percent. These optimists were not Pollyannas; they still had the same job description and the same performance expectations as their pessimistic colleagues. Except the glasses the optimists looked through were the ones that said success was imminent—the glass was half full.

Dr. Sonja Lyubomirsky is regarded in positive psychology circles as a leading researcher on optimism and happiness. She recently conducted a landmark meta-analysis reviewing over 200 peer academic studies to see whether there were any distinct linkages that rose to the top regarding work productivity and individual happiness.

At the conclusion of the study, Lyubomirsky showed that, on average, there is a 31 percent increase in productivity and a sales rise of a remarkable 37 percent in optimistic environments.

Despite the fact this research, in theory, is about workplace environments, we all "work" in some capacity—whether it is as a volunteer, conducting family affairs, building community relationships, involvement in special interest groups, in fact, anything we do that requires us to lead a productive life.

Ultimately, the goal is to lead not only a productive life but one that is also a life of compassion. Clearly there is much wisdom to reflect on regarding leading our own lives with an optimistic self-assessment where we can see others and events with more hopefulness and positive anticipation. And, when there is a sense of harmony and peacefulness inside ourselves, we then can live and work more in harmony and peace with those around us.

Optimism is What Optimism Does

One of the finest movies I have ever watched is *Forrest Gump*. Sitting on a park bench on a sunny day, Forrest Gump's mother—played impeccably by Sally Field—looks at her son and, with parental wisdom, states, "Stupid is as stupid does."

You could take this line and insert any word to replace "stupid"—the most famous version of this being, "Happy is as happy does."

I will make my own contribution by offering that, "Optimism is as optimism does." In essence, what we put out we get back. In my second book, *Four Generations One Workplace: Sharing in the Information Age,* I discuss the importance of creating supportive workplaces where people grow and reach their potential.

One way to do this is by making a conscious effort to increase the positive exchanges we have in relation to those around us. In other words, changing the number of positive and negative interactions in your work or life so the positives outweigh the negatives.

In 1999, Dr. Marcial Losada, then Director of the Center for Advanced Research in Ann Arbor, Michigan, began studying work teams to see how their interactions would impact the productivity of a group.

Teams were observed by counting the number of positive and negative interactions through both verbal and non-verbal cues passing through the group. After years of observation, the researchers were able to conclude that, in order to be a thriving team, there must be three positive interactions to every negative interaction as a minimum—with an optimal five-to-one ratio to ensure the team flourishes.

The average workplace has a reversal of this, with six negatives on average for every one positive. With my work with teams over the years, I would definitely support this average as well.

The conclusion based on these studies is easy to implement: change the ratio, and the team will change and so will productivity.

From my vantage point, I can draw further conclusions. Negative interactions denote a lack of compassion in operation among team members, as well as a lack of optimism and collaboration regarding the outcome of an exchange. Instead, it would seem that, where negative interactions dominate, the teams have "learned pessimism" and, in effect, learned to be powerless to change the dynamics of their situations. They have forgotten the quality of optimism and the resiliency it provides. These ramifications attest to the urgent need to inculcate the practice of compassionate optimism in our workplaces.

Regardless of the setting, in order for a cohort of people to arrive at the tipping point of creating a society of compassion—where bullying, sarcasm, distrust, disrespect, apathy, gossip, and alienation come to an end—we must begin at the very basics: reflecting on what messages we are sending out to others, verbally and non-verbally.

Challenge yourself to begin by being a silent observer of those around you. Counting the positive and negative interactions is a great place to begin. If you reflect on the people you spend the most time with, in counting interactions you will uncover both raw gold and the sludge in which it's immersed, and further understand that which you want to cultivate within yourself.

The Golden Ratio

Dr. John Gottman, professor emeritus at the University of Washington and author of *The Seven Principles for Making Marriage Work*, has spent years observing couples in his "Love Lab." He and his colleagues also note verbal and non-verbal exchanges in order to see if patterns emerge concerning the positive-to-negative ratio and if there is a correlation to successful relationships.

Gottman is known as someone who can predict with 91 percent accuracy whether a couple will stay happily together or will "cascade their way to divorce" as he refers to it. The cascade occurs once a couple reaches a one-part-positive-to-one-part-negative interaction level.

Gottman clarifies the success formula by adding, "Happily married couples aren't smarter, richer, or more psychologically astute than others. But in their day-to-day lives, they have hit upon a dynamic that keeps their negative thoughts and feelings about each other from overwhelming their positive ones." Interestingly, his research indicated the ratio teams require to thrive (five positive interactions to every one negative) is the same for relationships.

Positive Tickets

My dear colleague Ward Clapham knows the value of positive-to-negative ratios in his challenging work.

He has proudly served for over 30 years in the Royal Canadian Mounted Police. When he was asked to take command of the third-largest detachment in Canada, he also inherited the traditional command and control lexicon of law enforcement. When you know Ward, you know that he willingly steps out of the box in order to make a difference.

Ward submitted this excerpt from his book, *Lead Big: Discovering the Upside of Unconventional Leadership*, to share with others how important positive interactions and optimism are in order to make a difference in the life of an individual and a community.

> While on a routine patrol, I came across one of our well-known troubled youth hanging outside the local arcade. I'll call him Steve. Steve was 15 years old and had a checkered past, to say the least. He had been arrested multiple times for underage drinking, and I had busted him just two weeks previously for possession of stolen property. When I saw him that night, he wasn't doing anything wrong—yet. So I decided to try something different.
>
> "Hey, Steve," I said. "What're you doing?"
>
> "Nothing, officer; just hanging out," Steve said.
>
> "Steve, I have a deal for you tonight. How about going swimming or skating? I am going to give you a free pass—a Positive Ticket."
>
> "You're not going to shake me down again?"
>
> "No, it's your lucky night. I actually think you are a great kid; you just need a second chance. And tonight I am going to give you a break." I handed him a ticket. Something caught my attention as Steve looked at the Positive Ticket. He seemed confused, and I sensed that he couldn't read it very well. So I said, "Use this ticket to go to the indoor water park tonight. I hear the water slides are awesome."
>
> I saw Steve a few days later. We chatted about his evening at the water park. After some time, he basically admitted he couldn't read and he was having great difficulty in school. I told him about an after-school program to help

him with his reading. I explained that I wanted him to look into the program because his only other real option was getting continuously busted by me and ending up in jail for a long, long time. I helped him get into the reading program, and he started attending regularly. A few weeks later, Steve asked me for another Positive Ticket. He told me he wanted to keep this one as a reminder to stay on the good side of the law. I don't think anyone had ever told him before that he mattered—that he was a good kid. I gave him another ticket and wrote on it, "Steve, I'm Proud of You!" and signed it. Steve began to do better in school. His self-confidence grew. He got a job at a local store. Now, Steve is in college and working part-time. His problems with the law have ended. I ran into Steve not too long ago. With a big smile on his face, he said, "Thanks for believing in me." As the relationships between my officers and the youth improved, trust increased as well.

Most of the officers no longer viewed the kids as a nuisance or troublemakers, and most youth didn't view the police as "hunters" or some unknown cop. The kids began trusting us. They wanted to talk to an officer; they wanted to hang out; they wanted, of course, to get Positive Tickets. The kids were excited to show they were being good. In my town, it became cool to be good. The Richmond RCMP Detachment was handing out 40,000 Positive Tickets a year (a three-to-one ratio compared to negative or violation tickets). As a result of several youth prevention initiatives, including Positive Tickets, our youth-related service calls dropped by almost 50 percent, keeping more than 1,000 youth out of the juvenile justice system.

In this case, taking judgment out and inserting compassionate optimism is reaching out to one kid with one

Positive Ticket at a time. Add up the positive reinforcement rather than traditional enforcement and you get an entirely different kind of police backup. Although Ward is no longer responsible for this detachment, his results are so notable that police departments around the world have come to view his former squad and their effect on the community. Ward closed by sharing what he found most important.

> The part that makes it worthwhile is pulling into a parking lot full of kids; instead of running away from me, they swarm me. The rewarding part is driving down the street, looking out my window at some kids, and having them wave at me. The real result is seeing a youth who was on the edge of crime now far from it because he or she made a friend with one of my officers through Positive Tickets. The payoff is that kids don't feel I am hunting them anymore; they see me as a friend.

And, I will add, a compassionate and optimistic friend.

Pay it Forward

In the end, it is all about paying it forward; it is all about down-to-earth gratitude that increases the circle of compassionate optimism. What Ward did through the Positive Ticketing program stems back to making people feel valued, respected, and heard—one kid at a time. Those peaks and valleys, those ghosts and ogres, give us the tools to be kind and compassionate and then to do something optimistic—to create our own circles of outreach; otherwise, the lesson was only for us and the circle becomes smaller.

Edith, a volunteer coordinator at a large seniors' retirement home, wrote to me that there is a volunteer who faithfully brings a dozen roses to the home once a month and they are then given to a resident who would welcome receiving the colorful bouquet. The volunteer wishes to remain completely anonymous.

"She is a very humble lady," Edith comments, "and remembers when she was experiencing a down time, and someone did the same thing for her. She gets her reward when she is told how surprised and happy the resident was to receive the roses and it makes her day!"

This unknown volunteer pays it forward to a complete stranger every month. And yet, are they strangers to one another? I am not so certain. As the giver recalls her own vulnerability and the benevolence she experienced and that inspires her now, I am inclined to think that the giver and receiver have much in common; there is a shared empathy—the giver's isolation was broken by someone's compassion and hope and now she does the same.

Kathleen spoke earlier of contagious compassion—of hoping that by acting with compassion, she might move someone else to do the same. The gift of roses by the unknown volunteer is a monthly reminder to us all of what is most important in life: to pay it forward lest we forget the gifts we have received; to keep front and center the joy of remaining optimistic and the loving-kindness of compassion.

The Greatest of Zeal

Edith submitted a second contribution, from her own experience this time. Her church stewardship committee decided to do a community outreach event at a local inner city Mission and make meals for 400 homeless men and women. The event just happened to fall on Valentine's Day.

> We donated $1,000 to purchase the ingredients and we had 10 volunteers who assisted with preparation and serving of the meal. We had asked the center if we could leave something for them, and were told that we had to have 400 of whatever because we couldn't miss anyone out.
> So, I computer-generated 400 pink valentines and bought 400 red foil-covered chocolate hearts at the dollar store because it was cost effective. As each street person came through the line for their food, I was at the end of the food line with my basket of hearts and valentines and each person lit up when they received the little acknowledgement.
> One particular gentleman, obviously down on his luck for a very long time, was watching what I was doing as he proceeded through the line. When he got to me, I handed him the items, and said, "Happy Valentine's Day."

> He smiled at me with a toothless grin, and his beautiful eyes crinkled at the corners.
>
> He said, "Will you?"
>
> I said, "Will I what?" to which he responded, "Be my Valentine?"
>
> I was taken aback, and said "Sure!"
>
> He said, "Thank you—you made my day!" He had the most beautiful eyes, and I will never forget that moment.
>
> We had been told by staff that the valentines would probably end up crumpled up on the floor or on their dirty dishes. However, at clean-up, there were very few left behind and I felt humbled that a gesture so small would have such a large impact on so many.

Although Edith had been forewarned that her efforts to craft the delicate paper valentines would likely end up in the recycle bin, she was not dissuaded from her optimistic path. If even one person kept his valentine, it was worth the endeavor.

Edith showed that compassionate optimism is about taking responsibility for the energy and vitality you bring to the space surrounding you. What kind of optimistic force do you bring to your space, whether at home, work, a coffee shop, or mall? Acting with compassion has a way of yanking us out of ourselves and into the spirit of another—it creates a split second of sub-atomic unification, a hum that resonates in the very fibers of our beings.

When optimism is applied to compassion, we take off our shoes and slip yours on—even if they fit ever so tightly and awkwardly. When we hear the call, "Will you be my Valentine?" we answer, "Sure!" with the greatest of loving zeal.

Renewing Optimism through Gratitude

To cultivate and keep alive optimism we must also cultivate and keep alive gratitude. It is the indescribable touchpoint where the receiver acknowledges the giver, even if the giver is never aware of this acknowledgement. Gratitude is an innermost crossing for both to discover. From world faith traditions to modern-day philosophers, gratitude has been taught from the pulpit and inside temples, discussed passionately in philosopher cafés, and studied as mainstream psychology.

"Gratitude unlocks the fullness of life," author Melody Beattie calls to mind. "It turns what we have into enough, and more. It turns denial into acceptance, chaos to order, confusions to clarity. It can turn a meal into a feast, a house into a home, a stranger into

> When someone does something good, applaud!
> You will make two people happy.
>
> Samuel Goldwyn

a friend. Gratitude makes sense of our past, brings peace for today, and creates a vision for tomorrow."

These are thoughtful words coming from someone who has been through more than an adequate amount of pain in her lifetime and has come out on the other side positive. Beattie chose the path of a compassionate optimistic and moved triumphantly past life hurdles such as sexual abuse, addictions, and depression by finding the gifts in her experience. She then used her wisdom to get in touch with others by sharing her own authentic stories recorded throughout her 15 books and has helped others come to terms with codependency to triumph over their tragedies.

If this concept of gratitude as a healer resonates with you, then cultivating a more positive outlook is crucial by beginning with the simple act of recognizing those people and events that you indeed appreciate. The practice of being appreciative may seem unsophisticated and even far too easy to apply—and for some it may well be—however, for the vast majority, being grateful is not so easy, and, in some circles, may even be seen as a weakness.

Some may have a perception that expressing gratitude is exposing an Achilles heel, a defect so great that, if we acknowledge another person for listening to our troubles, for giving us a hand up, or for opening a career door, we are somehow flawed and indebted to them. We are conditioned to believe that vulnerable people get hurt more. Therefore, the message is to not admit vulnerability, to not need compassion. Yet, gratitude does not mean that anyone is owed anything. If we believe this, then it diminishes the sincerity of the act of thankfulness. There is no debt to be repaid, no score to keep, no measurement to follow.

A Habit of Gratitude

Dr. Albert Schweitzer, recipient of the 1952 Nobel Peace Prize, shares his view on embracing gratitude—knowing that we will all go through times when our own light dims and that "it is rekindled by a spark from another person. Each of us has cause to think with deep gratitude of those who have lighted the flame within us."

Reg has been an entrepreneur the majority of his working life and shared with me how, in the early stages of his career, he was fortunate to be hired as a salesperson by a young, progressive company that was owned by two partners who were very different from one another both in skills and personalities.

> I was fairly new in the process of my conscious personal development at the time and both of these men quickly became mentors to me. In different yet powerful ways, each helped shape me into the person I was to be-

come. In the 11 years under their employ I grew significantly, both personally and professionally, taking on increasing roles of responsibility and eventually leading to an opportunity to own my own business.

Years later I sold my business interests, retired from the industry, and set out on a new career path of creating and presenting personal and professional development programs. Over time my former bosses and I fell out of contact, until a few years later, while travelling home from one of these events, it struck me that I had told the story of these two men and their positive influence on me perhaps a hundred times to participants in my programs, yet I had never expressed it to them personally. That realization shocked me!

Late that same evening I sat down and wrote out a greeting card to each of them, sharing what they had meant to me and how much they had impacted my life. Several days later, I received a phone call from one of these two gentlemen and he shared with me that, for a number of years he had been suffering from a debilitating disease similar to MS. When my card arrived he had been bedridden for three consecutive days and was in a very down emotional state. He was almost in tears as he told me how much my words meant to him and how much they had lifted him up. This experience reinforced to me just how much a few minutes invested in expressing gratitude, appreciation, respect, admiration, or encouragement can mean to another human being.

In our interview, Reg shared with me that it is important for him to "give thought to the people he is grateful for." Taking this call for action to the finite level he committed himself from that time forward to send out a minimum of one card per day to someone, somewhere to express his appreciation.

Reg's advice to get people started on a habit of gratitude is to make a commitment of sending out one greeting card per day for 30 days. His advice is simple: "Many people say they don't have 30 friends to complete this exercise. Look around your community, your neighborhood, the corner grocery store, your local politicians. Begin acknowledging someone that stands for something you believe in." Reg added, "People have trouble speaking their thoughts but can write it more easily. You can be more articulate and it is safer to express yourself when you send a meaningful card."

He also makes a very good point that cards should be sent out not only to those we know and appreciate. It is important to also acknowledge the people who may be annoying to us in some way, because they are also our teachers. Our learning is in the effort of moving past the irritation to see the good they have done and the contribution they have made in your life and the lives of others. Therein lies a great challenge in itself, I would say. It would be essential to make certain a portion of the 30 people chosen also include some of these folks—for our own benefit as well as theirs. He also suggests sending cards out to people to remind them of their potential—of who they can be because of something you see in them.

Count Your Blessings—Name Them One by One

Through experience, Reg knows how vital it is to the human spirit to remain, for as large an amount of time as possible, in a place of gratitude, by counting blessings one person and one acknowledgement at a time. For some, this subtitle may remind you of a hymn that sounds familiar, or perhaps it is a way in which you live your life naturally or would like to in the future.

The act of gratitude and its impact on changing one's life can actually be measured according to Dr. Robert Emmons, a professor and researcher at the University of California, Davis, who studies the psychology of gratitude and personal goals in relation to one's happiness and well-being. Admittedly, as I searched for actions that build the optimism muscle, I was surprised that the vast majority of research returned to what Reg had already implied and practiced in his life—appreciation and gratitude.

One way to begin this journey toward enhancing optimism is to take affirmative action in the written word. Dr. Emmons's research validates the power of keeping a gratitude journal.

This finding surprised me, as I had been expecting science to tell me something deep and difficult, not inviting and practical. Firstly, let go of the notion of a teenage girl's diary filled with raw and youthful emotions, secured with a keyed lock, and clandestinely placed in a drawer filled with socks. Journaling has been around for centuries—since the advent of papyrus, symbols, and basic writing instruments.

In relation to how journaling improves our ability to be grateful, however, it is a relatively fresh science. Research indicates that making written note of the positives in life through weekly accounting seemingly shores up individuals to see the world around them more optimistically. Those who journal faithfully report fewer physical symptoms, less depression and anxiety, and they tend to create an expanded freedom to progress toward personal goals. Daily gratitude appears to swing open the door for acts of generosity and compassion to others.

Could something as unadorned as a blank book and taking as little as 10 minutes a day make such a difference in our lives and the lives of others? Dr. Emmons says, "People are 25 percent happier and more energetic if they keep gratitude journals, have 20 percent less envy and resentment, sleep 10 percent longer each night and wake up 15 percent more refreshed, exercise 33 percent more, and show a 10 percent drop in blood pressure compared to persons who are not keeping these journals."

Once again, the "happiness" word surfaces and the investment of giving out compassionate optimism comes back to us tenfold. As I write this, I am reminded of the man in the blue maintenance uniform who sparked my journey. At the end of sharing his story, he offered gratitude to his colleagues by saying, "I want to thank some of the people in this room who have shown me how to do this because I learned from watching you for years."

Journaling toward Gratitude

I would hope that those stellar findings entice you to begin a journal or start a list of what blessings adorn your life. This method of offering up 10 minutes a day toward stating what we are grateful for can be applied to our lives both personally and professionally.

In a workplace setting, before the world of consulting, I managed human resources departments in three different organizations. To each team, I have recommended gratitude journals for the reason that it is all too easy, within the sterile world of business, to lose sight of the positive work we do—especially when businesses emphasize a monthly cycle... and then you move on with the pressures of the next 30 days.

By formulating weekly gratitude and placing emphasis on the positive, we balance any ratios that are out of kilter and even change them—we bring the positive forward and make the negative recede, taking the back seat it deserves.

Taking time to acknowledge at least one daily positive in writing is optimal. Opening a meeting with gratitude toward a person or circumstance is a great way to stay connected to the higher purpose of one's work.

Every job has something to be grateful for—great people, a near accident miss, a department success, marriages and births, even a miracle here or there. Win/win situations abound across businesses if we slow down long enough to see them. Many are subtle and become some of the most important ones—but get missed while we chase the big successes. We get what we see, but are we seeing as pessimists or optimists? Based on the research, cultivating an optimistic approach makes us come out on top every time.

As a college educator, I instruct in the business faculty and I adore my students' enthusiasm for just about everything that comes their way. Many component pieces of my own research in and around this topic of optimism have been conducted annually over the past four years with students during their midterm exam.

Over a three-week period, students are requested to journal their silent observations of the positive-to-negative interactions within their professional and personal relationships. The success of the exercise is for them to compartmentalize the positives and negatives into weekly segments so they are watching and listening for verbal and non-verbal cues in each category for the entire week—with no one being aware that they are observing.

Along the way, students are expected to record the journey of what they have witnessed and felt physically, emotionally, and mentally during each week and then to write a paper on their most teachable moment of clarity. The results are reflective and genuinely thoughtful as the students express how focusing exclusively on either the positives or negatives in their life each week had a physiological and emotional effect on them based on what they spent their time immersed in.

The age-old lesson of "you are what you think" is impossible to teach, coach, lecture, or train, and remains a theory without those experiential components. As their teacher, my goal is to get the students to realize how much influence their environment has on them—and, of course, how much influence they have in return.

This assignment may be low-tech; nevertheless, it is unquestionably one with a high touch impact, with 95 percent of students stating that this test has altered their life in a positive way.

Optimism, just like pessimism, is a learned behavior and a choice that requires effort. And, if we are not vigilant in which way we lean, then we take on what is the strongest propensity around us—we revert to our "resting place."

If you enjoy experiential learning, then undertaking this assignment yourself will be beneficial. Better yet, challenge a group to carry out the exercise. Afterward, hold an authentic dialogue on each week's observations and share the influence you noticed as you looked through only one of two lenses, and how a specific lens of either positive or negative can literally change your view. You may notice that the world around us, whether pessimistic or optimistic, is greatly influenced by how we interact with one another, including how we reference people, objects, events, and places.

Striving to nurture more skills as a compassionate optimist requires some effort. As with my students, I will offer up the same recommendation I give to them. Based on all the current research on improving an optimistic outlook, acknowledging what you are thankful for is still the most effective approach. And the simplest and most effective means of doing so is keeping a journal.

When journaling, do not think you need to write your day's account verbatim. A list of what you are grateful for can be in bulleted format or written in a couple of short, expressive sentences—or even a lengthy paragraph, depending upon your style. It can be a doodle or cartoon, an image that captures the event or feeling.

Keep in mind that it is better to write three things a week that are deeply meaningful to you than to routinely record a number per day. Don't make recording gratitude a mindless chore, something you have to do rather than want to do.

Whatever you do record, take the time to reflect on it. Visualize it and hold it dear to you as a positive memory, remembering that this is not a to-do list for you to complete—it is a sacred memory you want to capture. So savor each one and reminisce with it.

The bonus gift of capturing these written gratitude words through journaling also allows an opportunity to archive your joys so as to be able to refer back to them when going through a time period where you may be feeling a little less than optimistic. In "A Science," I suggested you might jumpstart your compassionate self and produce more oxytocin by recalling happy memories. A gratitude journal may do the same and jumpstart your optimism when times are less than ideal.

To be able to return to and recall all those areas of gratitude can and will be a gift to help turn you around when you are heading down the wrong road. As an author, I know this as fact—writing is healing and energizing for me because I get to place my stories of gratitude into writing.

Writing helps us organize our thoughts, stop, and ponder, and encourages us to take inventory rather than simply losing track of blessings that come our way and get eaten up with the busyness of life. The value of paying attention to what is good in life is like turning the corner to a more optimistic street to walk down, a street that is brightly illuminated.

You Are What You Write

When all the research is accounted for and delved into, there is no right or wrong way to begin or maintain a gratitude journal. The right way is *your* way; it is the way that feels true to you when pen is put to paper.

At the beginning of your day or at the end—it makes no difference any more than choosing to write your thoughts on a digital device, a notebook, or napkin. The key to unlock this sacred door of gratitude is merely the act of initiation—noting the positives in your life, honoring them, and at the same time, changing the ratio regarding the number of negative and positive interactions you have with others.

We get what we seek and we are what we write.

> An aboriginal elder was speaking to his young grandson. He said, "Grandson, I feel as if I have two wolves fighting in my heart. One wolf is angry and hurtful. The other wolf is loving and compassionate."
>
> The grandson asked him, "Grandfather, which wolf will win the fight in your heart?"
>
> The wise elder answered, "The one I feed."

Acknowledging with Gratitude

On this journey to conjoin the words compassion and optimism I have come to realize that all it takes is someone giving us a loving push. We get busy and we forget what we intuitively already know—that we are compassionate, generous, and positive individuals.

When facilitating workshops, I ask participants to slow down for a moment—to leave work behind them and reminisce with gratitude on the people and events that have touched their lives with joy, laughter, encouragement, unconditional friendship, and love... regardless of how brief an encounter.

Participants are given a blank paper frame and asked to create an inner picture with names and memorable moments in time. The list may include teachers who have aided them to succeed in school; friends who have been there unconditionally; colleagues who made them feel valued, respected, and heard; and family who have been role models and heroes.

In addition, I ask them to reflect on individuals who just crossed their path at an unexpected, yet perfect, moment. Many may have been honored to witness something beautiful, may have been the recipient of a kindhearted act, a smile, a comment, or a gesture that brightened their day. If we open our eyes wide enough, we'll recognize that our world is full of earth angels crossing our paths daily.

Recently, while facilitating an all-day workshop on compassion for 200 leaders, I was allowing time for reflection on gratitude. As storytelling began at each table, Neil, the audiovisual technician hired for the event, approached me and asked if I had a moment for him to show me something.

Thinking there might be a technical problem, I made my way over to his station. "There is something I want you to see," Neil said. "I have worked for this company for close to two years and I really like my job. But I know if it weren't for two guys here who trained me on everything they know that I wouldn't have been able to keep it. I am always telling myself that I should write a letter to both of them and thank them or that I should tell the boss how much I appreciate what these guys have done for me. I have been sitting back here listening to what you had to say and I wanted to show you the letter that I just wrote during this part of the session. I am going to mail it to both of them tomorrow and I am going to tell my boss, as well. It was important for me to tell you that I heard you and I finally did something about it."

A beaming Neil then opened and shared an email full of praise and acknowledgement of his colleagues. It was a beautiful reminder to me of how powerful gratitude is and how important it is that we take that first step forward. It also reminded me that unknowingly we may touch someone's heart and in that powerful circle of reciprocity, they will be inspired to reach out and touch someone else.

Compassion and optimism are not distant relatives who don't speak to each other; they are confidants on a quest to co-create and cooperate. Science has offered us a means by which we may understand that we truly do have the opportunity to choose. As the wise elder said, what we feed and nurture is what will live in our hearts.

Compassionate optimism is a conscious choice we make to enjoy life and take action—not tomorrow, but today.

Chapter 5

Compassionate Purpose

The purpose of life is not to be happy.
It is to be useful, to be honorable, to be compassionate,
to have it make some difference that you have lived and lived well.

Ralph Waldo Emerson

It takes no more time to see the good side of life than to see the bad.

Jimmy Buffett

"Olivia!" I could hear my name being called—more like barked—across a sea of people. I felt like a six-year-old preparing for a reprimand, as my short experience here at Mother Teresa's told me something was coming.

Under the morning sunshine in New Delhi, I was happily applying fingernail polish to a woman whose left hand was so gnarled it curved under her palm. That didn't stop her from wanting both hands to be a perfect match. A dozen more women were gathered in the garden, eagerly waiting their turn. The residents loved to have their nails colored in bright neon pinks, reds, and oranges, meticulously choosing just the right color to match their equally bright saris.

I could not speak their language, and so, for me, painting finger and toe nails was a time of bonding with the residents. We were women from different life circumstances but our connection was our mutual admiration for a well-manicured hand. Sharing smiles and simple pleasures took the place of the common language we lacked. There were no words, no expectations, no struggle to pantomime—this time in the garden was precious.

"Olivia, go NOW. Clean toilets."

I froze midway through applying ruby red polish and looked up. My first reaction was disbelief. *You want me to do what?* I thought sarcastically. *No, really, she must be kidding me, right?* This time with a tad more anxiety.

I hadn't envisioned this when I first set out on my quest to explore compassion in action. I was paralyzed at the thought of leaving this idyll in the garden to clean the dreadfully dingy cement washrooms.

"Olivia!"

Once again the call rang out like a bell summoning me—this time, with a firmer tone. For the first time in my life, I wished someone didn't remember my name or, better yet, I had another one.

Purpose with Paint, Polish and Pancakes

We all run into those moments, don't we? Whether it's a task we don't like or an idea of ourselves that is challenged, we find ourselves suddenly taken over by a balky mule that kicks its heels in protest.

The call to clean toilets was such a moment for me. It didn't fit in with my idea of the role I played at the Home and it wasn't part of what I saw as my job description. I don't think I had actually even realized I had encumbered myself that way, and yet I had.

Job description, by definition, means "the general tasks, duties, and responsibilities" one is assigned to complete. Whether you work in a large or small company, your role is defined by your job description. Where you sit; whether you have a desk, a cubicle, or office; whether you instruct or are instructed; whether you advise, consult, or assist: your job description is like a jacket you put on when you walk in the door of your work. Some wear this jacket with pride and have difficulty taking it off, while others earnestly wait to place it back on its hanger at the end of the day and walk away.

It is often a jacket we put on without any consideration of how it fits. Does it fit like a straitjacket—restricting confining? Do you wear this jacket as

> Deprived of meaningful work, men and women lose their reason for existence; they go stark, raving mad.
>
> Fyodor Dostoevsky

though someone had made it entirely for you? Does putting it on change your personality into someone you don't really intend or like to be?

Carl works in a paint store. It would be easy to see him as just another salesman and it would be just as easy for him to see you as another anonymous customer. But that's not his approach. Carl's view is: "Color is much more than paint. It can elevate moods and make you feel better by just walking into a room. Color can have a calming effect on adults and children and they have even experimented with it in hospitals, prisons, and schools. I believe that I am selling inspiration in a can and I make people happier."

What a gift Carl brings to his encounters with each person who walks in that store. I am quite sure they leave with their own sense of purpose, imbued by Carl's passion and approach to what he does.

Kevin works in the maintenance and janitorial services department of a large hospital where he is responsible for maintaining the floors with an industrial rider floor polisher. When Kevin looks around, he sees people, not floors. He sees fathers and mothers and daughters and sons, friends and family members who are missing out on special holiday seasons during their stay at the hospital.

Kevin is meticulous in his work, but that's not what defines him. What defines him is the compassionate purpose he brings to his job. For every major holiday, Kevin decorates his rider polisher—and sometimes even himself. He is warm and sensitive to different cultural beliefs, so he is constantly changing the decoration on his polisher. He brings smiles, and the healing balm that comes from smiling, to all who see him as he goes about his work.

Patti is another who takes this inspiration into the workplace setting with her, making her purposeful in her daily tasks. Patti loves her work in foodservice at a small rural hospital where she takes a little extra time to make breakfast pancakes into little kittens for the children's ward. She says, "If I can take a little more time—make food look special—they will eat more and get healthier quicker."

No Borders or Boundaries

Sometimes we find our chance to practice compassionate purpose by doing something pleasant—like painting fingernails. Sometimes we find it in unexpected places by the way in which we sell products, polish floors, or make pancakes. Sometimes we must find it by cleaning toilets. Compassionate purpose is not about only doing the parts of our job or taking on tasks that we want to do, or taking on ones with feel-good outcomes.

The reality is that work and life are full of tasks that are not sweet; they are mundane, not considered "sexy," and understandably, no one else may want to do them. Yet, purposeful work is about the moment you are in now—not one moment before or one moment after. That is what I was encountering at Mother Teresa's Home in New Delhi.

The latrine had eight toilets—two traditional Western toilets and six Indian "squat toilets," which are floor mounted with feet grates on either side for squatting rather than sitting. These toilets were used multiple times a day by well over a hundred women residents of the Home suffering from ailments affecting either their health or their mental well-being—and they came with their own array of competencies and hygiene.

I reluctantly left my happy post as a nail painter and went to the Sister in question. I suggested I was in the middle of an important task. She promptly replied that toilets were more important than nail polish.

Bless her heart, but if you have ever tried to negotiate with a Catholic nun, you will know this conversation ended abruptly. Without further ado, the Sister pointed me in the direction of my assignment.

I wondered how I could do this task without a face mask and thought of hiding somewhere on the grounds until it was time to leave. However, I knew the Sister would eventually track me down and likely make me do this task two days in a row.

My expectations had run aground on the hard granite floor at Mother Teresa's. I had found a boundary I needed to cross, and quickly.

As an emergency room nurse, Lynn holds to the practice of breaking down all boundaries, letting go of judgments, and expecting nothing in return.

> It doesn't see skin color, socioeconomic status, or faith. Compassion sees through matted hair, bug-infested bodies, and foul odors, and rises above angry words, spitting, and non-verbal scowls. Compassion is a gift that one bestows on another with no expectations of a favor in return and is accepting the opportunity to bring a small glimmer of peace to a person in need.

Lynn has spent 16 years becoming intimate with the higher purpose of her work and learning how compassion is at its heart, especially within challenging situations. Here is her unique snapshot of various experiences where compassionate purpose has been in action for her:

> Holding the hand of a woman having a miscarriage • Giving a bath to an intoxicated man covered in feces • Taking the initiative to find an extra large wheel-

> chair for an obese man who is clearly uncomfortable in the standard-sized chair • Crying with a mother who lost her two-year-old daughter after a tragic accident • Providing a winter coat to a homeless man looking to keep warm • Staying stretcherside with a frail, elderly woman because you don't want her to die alone • Helping a young mother make countless phone calls until she finds a ride home; you know if she walks, every joint in her ailing body will hurt • Telling an elderly man he can spend the night in the waiting room because he has nowhere else to go • Calling a patient the next day, because your heart wants to know the person is feeling better • Sitting in silence with a family after their loved one was just diagnosed with cancer

I walked over to the washroom. A resident was already at work, washing down the gray concrete shower walls. I decided to start by helping her.

Her name was Nita. I told her my name was Liv—that's my nickname, and it was much easier for residents to pronounce than my real name. She could not speak English and I could not speak Hindi. Exchanging names was the end of our verbal conversation, but it was not the end of our communication.

Both bathing and cleaning at the Home is done with hand towels cut in squares from coarse burlap rice sacks. They are as rough as a scrub brush. Nita showed me where to find them. Then she showed me how to clean the walls and floors of the showers and, together, we set to work.

Nita laughed at me because, at times, I had more disinfectant soapy water on me than on the walls. We smiled at each other a lot while working together.

Eventually, I made my way to the toilets.

We Could Be on Either Side

Lynn's snapshot reminded me of the frailty of so many at Mother Teresa's, and indeed, the frailty of so many of our own here at home. Lynn reminded me that any of us, at any time, could find ourselves in need of someone's care. We could be family whose loved one has just received a frightening diagnosis. We could be the obese man, the woman who just had a miscarriage or lost a child to an accident, or we could be the homeless man.

We may not find our compassionate purpose at once or every time we are called upon to bring it to what we are doing, but there are opportunities around us every day to do so. When we dare to put ourselves in someone else's shoes for even a moment of time, we are practicing compassionate purpose.

When I see a couple arguing, a parent berating a child, a

> Happiness comes when we test our skills towards some meaningful purpose.
>
> John Stossel

customer angry with a clerk, I see those who are unaware that it is possible to address problems and issues with compassionate purpose. That responding to anger with anger, or to crying with impatience, denies ourselves an opportunity to look into the eyes of another and see the hurt that compels her behavior. We may not be able to fix it, but we do not need to leap into the mire and respond in kind. Perhaps we can be like Carl at the paint store and offer inspiration; we can bring compassion forward and begin a cycle of reciprocity.

There is much wisdom found in the words of the Swiss 19th-century philosopher and poet Henri-Frédéric Amiel, who wrote: "Life is short and we have never too much time for gladdening the hearts of those who are traveling the dark journey with us. Oh be swift to love, make haste to be kind."

Finding Your "Is"

Some would argue that not every "job" can be meaningful. If you believe that work is only about completing a series of tasks, then this paradigm may very well be correct. There are scores of mundane, unpleasant, or repetitive tasks within work, home, school, and even the volunteer community, yet each one is crucial to keeping the wheels of our organized lives churning. However, purposeful work has little to do with the actual tasks or duties of the work, but, rather, the attitude in how the work tasks are accomplished.

Purpose comes wrapped up in one's approach to what one does, how one shows up, and how one "is."

We live in a culture that celebrates winning and consumption and financial success, yet the extreme end of these trappings is available to only a few, and we believe we are entitled to them. I have come across so much subjective and objective evidence through my career and research that I am of the mind that we cannot wait for someone to generously hand out heaping plates of meaningful work, whether it is in our personal lives or our professions.

There simply are not enough "dream" or "cool" jobs—or even, for that matter, "dream lives"—to go around. However, we do have the possibility to empower ourselves. We can show up and create the cool job within the job itself. We can show up and create the dream life within the life we have been given.

I know this firsthand because I started my career in entry-level retail, and I clearly remember being in my 20s as a convenience store assistant manager making $7.50 an hour and thinking, "I would do this job for free because I love it so much." When I actually analyzed why I felt that way, it was because it had nothing to do with the tasks, and everything to do with who the tasks were for—the customer. Once I understood that, I was able to duplicate the mind-set by being very conscious for whom I did my work, regardless of what positions I held. I was able to generate my own sense of engagement.

Polly has found her "is" while employed as an administrator and a member of the faculty of an American university. She writes regarding holding compassion as one of her highest values and expresses how she blends together what she embraces so dearly with her daily work.

> I feel it's important to create a holding environment where faculty, students, and staff can feel, experience, give, and experiment with compassion. As an advisor and coach of many faculty members, I use compassion to help individuals become the best people they can become. My strategies of listening, gently pushing people to go beyond what they thought they were capable of, and helping people to live in their reality while setting new visions is all part of my compassionate leadership style.

Compassionate purpose is woven into her job description—not by her employer, but by Polly herself. It is her way of bringing engagement and meaning to what she does.

It behooves us all to look at our own span of control and to take inventory of the responsibility and accountability inherent in our work process. You may not have control over the description per se, but you surely do over the attitude you approach it with, whether it be optimistic or pessimistic, compassionate or callous. I am certain that no one can take your ability to choose your feelings and outlook from you.

In my work, I have lost track of the number of individuals who appear to enjoy the most advantageous job, and yet there is not an ounce of engagement emanating from them. On the other end of the spectrum, I have seen those who don't have dream jobs, but who find meaning and purpose in what they do—often they radiate something so special, others desire to be in their presence. Simple math says it's not the job—it's the person who holds the job. Whether that job is raising your family, cleaning tables in a restaurant, or running the IT department—it matters not.

Crysta allowed her "is" factor to surface while working in the insurance industry as an administrative clerk. It was the chilly month of February and closing in on Valentine's Day when she created packages of chocolates and goodies and distributed them to her colleagues with a note attached.

> On each valentine I wrote a message inside that said, "You have been gifted, return in kind in whatever manner your heart desires." It gives me joy. It opens up conversations with people on how kindness makes them feel. I feel richer by far than I have in many years. I feel there is a purpose to what I do and where I am that allows me to enjoy my sincere self. Something I have been hiding for a long time.

Take the time to unwrap your "is." Take the time to reflect on your purpose, whether at work or at home. Write down your answers or find someone with whom you can authentically share them.

What would be your "is" that makes people want to be in your presence? Do people have a little more joy because you came along today, or do they have a little less? Do you come to your life's work mean-spirited, show open disdain for your tasks, and treat others with disrespect? Or do you show up like Crysta and contribute emotionally, intellectually, and optimistically? Do you act from "we" rather than "me"?

I am a storyteller. A narrator of both my own stories and others with the intention to intertwine them into a picture in which everyone can find meaning. Many times I will use a fable, a parable, or a legend from various cultures and faith traditions to strengthen my message because we are all children at heart, are we not? And all can identify with the characters in the storyline. Here is a favorite of mine from India that weaves a tale of how important every task "is" and that every job counts and is meaningful if we choose to see this.

A Tale of Two Pots

A water bearer in India had two large ceramic pots, one hung on each end of a pole, which he carried across his neck. One of the pots had a crack running through the side of it. While the other pot was perfect, and always delivered a full portion of water at the end of the long walk from the stream to his house, the cracked pot arrived only half full. For a full two years this went on daily, with the bearer delivering only one and a half pots of water to his house. The perfect pot was proud of its accomplishments, perfect to the end for which it was made.

But the poor cracked pot was ashamed of its own imperfection, and miserable that it was able to accomplish only half of what it had been made to do.

After two years of what it perceived to be a bitter failure, the cracked pot finally spoke to the water bearer by the stream.

"I am ashamed of myself, and I want to apologize to you."

"Why?" asked the bearer. "What are you ashamed of?"

"For these past two years, I have only been able to deliver half my load of water because this crack in my side causes water to leak out all the way back to your house. Because of my flaws, you have to do all of this work, and you don't get full value from your efforts," the pot said.

The water bearer felt sorry for the old cracked pot, and in his compassion, he said, "As we return to the house, I want you to notice the beautiful flowers along the path."

Indeed, as they went up the hill, the old cracked pot took notice of the sun warming the beautiful flowers on the side of the path, and this cheered it some. But at the end of the trail, the cracked pot felt bad once again because it had leaked out half its load, and so again it apologized to the bearer for its failure.

The bearer said to the pot, "There is no need to apologize. Did you notice that there were flowers only on your side of the path, but not on the other pot's side? That's because I have always known about your flaw, and I took advantage of it. I planted flower seeds on your side of the path, and every day while we've walked back from the stream, you've watered them. For two years I have been able to pick these beautiful flowers to decorate my table. Without you being just the way you are, we would not have this beauty to grace our house."

The take-away message from this charming tale is how important it is to bring one's whole self to work: the good, the flaws, and the cracks in us all, because therein lies our "is" of what makes us who we are. Consciously wrapping our whole self in our work brings out our engagement to the task at hand—allowing flowers to bloom where we least expect them.

Mindful Purpose

After working with Nita, I made my way to the toilets with an entirely different disposition. I remembered for whom I cleaned those toilets. I remembered why they needed cleaning: for health and hygiene. I remembered what my purpose in coming to Mother Teresa's was.

Linda, a social worker, was placed in a heart wrenching situation and yet could see her way through it by never losing sight of who she did her work for, her contribution, and higher purpose. Linda's story begins as she enters the hospital room of a young woman and finds her sitting on the bed hunched over and looking very much alone, knowing that the inevitable is going to happen. Linda explains further:

> She looked up at me apprehensively with her big dark eyes. As I walked toward her, she began to cry. I calmly explained to her that because she had used just before the baby was born, as a child protection social worker, I had to remove the child from her custody. She was grief-stricken and I understood how much she really had wanted to stay clean and sober for her baby. I gently sat down beside her and stroked her hair. We sat on this little hospital bed as she cried with shame and sorrow. She wanted me to know that she had not wanted to hurt her child. She loved her baby. I told her I knew she loved her little girl. We sat together for a long time while she softly wept and told me how much she wanted to be a good mother.

As Linda has demonstrated, compassionate purpose is to lovingly see, then feel, your work so you can positively influence those in need while going about the difficult tasks that may be assigned to you.

> We sat together: the social worker who was taking her child and the mother who was brokenhearted. With compassion I acknowledge and validate someone's pain. With compassion I see past their behavior to their essence, their humanity. With compassion I sit with them so they are not alone with their pain. With compassion I respect their inner being. With compassion I love their spirit.

Purpose is present and may be woven into everything we do. It is the sustainable energy found, often hidden, in one's livelihood or daily life responsibilities, and it is an energy that is bequeathed to us in return. Linda cannot avoid what she has to do, and yet, does her work with love, non-judgment, and the intention of the highest good for all.

Edie

I wish you were with me when I met Edie. I was delivering a closing keynote on renewing the spirit of your work at an employability and career counseling conference. Waiting until everyone wishing to speak to me had left, a slight woman approached me and said, "Hi, my name is Edie; if you have a few minutes I would like to tell you how Beth changed forever how I look at my work."

"We can take as much time as you would like," I said as I motioned for us to sit down together at a nearby table.

Edie told me she had begun her career in long-term care as a nurse's aid worker, which she loved. She had been working at a couple of different homes part-time while she waited for a permanent role to open up at one of the locations.

Her story began on the first day of orientation with her manager who was showing Edie what her responsibilities would be. They walked into a resident's room...

> I can see her as vividly as I did all those years ago; she was such a lovely lady....Her name was Beth. She had lived a good life up to a rapid decline in her health over the last few years. Now she resided in a body that was contracted into a fetal position and she weighed no more than seventy pounds; Beth relied on us to do everything for her.
>
> During this first visit to her room I was hastily told that Beth had not spoken in four years, was deaf, and totally blind. "Get in and get out quickly. She won't even know you are here anyways and you have other people to take care of," I was instructed coldly.

I could see the terseness of this message disturbed Edie to her very center as she shook her head side to side, still disagreeing with her orders as she relived that long-ago conversation.

> I knew this was wrong. Something inside said this was a mistake because I had read reports about how patients in these conditions can still be communicated to, using vibrations through the skull bones. I made it a point that every time I entered Beth's room, I would greet her by cupping her face in my hands and putting my cheek to her cheek, hoping she could feel my vibration as I spoke to her. I would let her know I was there for her, it was time to eat, or that I was cleaning up her room.
>
> While doing my duties I would sing to her, tell her about my life and what was going on with my family. Whatever I said was always positive. I would tell her about events I had gone to, just about anything and everything. I would try to work extra quickly and, if I had a little time to spare, I would lie down beside her, put my cheek on hers so she could feel the vibration, and talk and sing to her. My colleagues thought I was crazy and told me I was wasting my time, but I didn't care. I knew for myself that I had to treat her with dignity and respect even if she never knew; it didn't matter because I knew it.

I recall commenting to Edie of what a truly beautiful illustration in relation to the capacity to see the higher calling of one's work. To not see the ailment in the person or to describe them as the deaf and blind woman in room 203, but rather to envision the life force, the quintessence of Beth—this was truly an immense gift she had. *There is no better example of true, purposeful work than this*, I thought.

Edie continued her narrative:

After working there for over four years I was fortunate to finally get offered a full-time position, but it was in a different town and it meant I would be moving in a few weeks. On my last day of work I made my rounds to each of the residents and let them know my good news.

Then I got to Beth's room and I was sad to have to tell her that I wouldn't see her again. I completed my duties quickly, knowing this would be the last time I would lay down beside her, my cheek to her cheek to share my news. I told her I would miss her and that she was special to me. I sang to her and then suddenly I felt something warm and wet on my face. I jumped off the bed, and ran around to look at Beth and saw there were tears running down her face. What? That is impossible! Without thinking about it I said, "Beth, can you hear me?" and, to my amazement, she said weakly, "Yes." How could that be? I was told she was deaf, blind, and couldn't speak. "Beth, how long have you been able to speak?" I asked. She must have had a sense of humor in her life because she replied with a smirk and a whisper, "Since I was two years old."

I needed to know why she was only speaking now, so I asked her. Her voice was very feeble, but she slowly managed to say, "Oh, Edie, don't stop singing. I couldn't have you leave without telling you how much you have meant to me since you came here. Everyone treats me like a lump in a bed, except you. You treat me as though I matter, and that you care, and I wanted to thank you." It took everything she had to be able to say this to me and it changed how I do my work forever.

Edie changed careers many years later. She is a woman who takes on her role as a career counselor with the same purpose and compassion as she did working in healthcare.

She told me that you never know what impact you are going to have, and therefore, you have to make every interaction count. "Follow your heart and also put people ahead of tasks," was Edie's final advice.

When Vocation meets Avocation

Implicit in Edie's story is the profound currency of vocation and avocation.

Each of us currently holds a vocation of some sort—either in the traditional sense of employment, in the vocation of raising a family, or even attending school full-time—which is a combination of skills, knowledge, and ability.

At the opposite of vocation's spectrum is its antonym, avocation. Avocation is a recreational or leisurely passion (and sometimes not so leisurely, depending upon the level of passion for it). Some may call avocation a hobby, talent, or gift that is cultivated outside the domain of one's regular vocation.

When vocation unites with avocation, there is a blending of skills and gifts that support having more meaningful work, making this aspiration of purpose easier to achieve. Crysta was able to bring her

> I would rather die a meaningful death than live a meaningless life.
>
> Corazon Aquino

passion for kindness to her role at work. Edie brought her profound belief in how precious each of us is and the extent to which she commits to that belief in her work.

You may know someone whose avocation for sports inspires them to organize a softball team for some fun competition; or someone who runs the social committee to create bonding amongst colleagues; and then there are those who are passionate about a particular charity and raise money to support its cause. Yet there are also many who keep their vocation and avocation separate—never blurring the line between the two, adhering to the widely held belief that what we do as our avocation should not cross into the workspace.

Today, this viewpoint is changing rapidly as the younger generations happily blur these lines and operate on a different set of values. Think of it this way; you cannot trespass across the boundaries of your vocation and avocation if the borders you are crossing are your own.

Sadly, there are many who believe that life is not about having an avocation, because there is no time. By their account, an avocation is reserved for the privileged—their own fate is reduced to a motto of "work hard, pay your dues, and do your time."

My friend Alisdair combines his vocation and avocation in a different way. He works as a full-time corporate training and development specialist and serves part-time as an Anglican deacon—his avocation.

Antoine de Saint-Exupéry worked as a pilot and, by avocation, was a writer. His classic, *The Little Prince,* has been translated into over 250 languages. Saint-Exupéry speaks of instilling a deeper work purpose in individuals by using the metaphor of building a boat.

He says not to tell people to simply "saw wood, stitch the sails, prepare the tools, and organize the work," but to set for themselves a compelling goal—something to visualize and involve them more deeply, such as, "make them long for setting sail" and to "travel to distant lands."

Bringing our whole selves to our work must include this deeper vision. It is a way of transforming the meaning of how we go about our daily routines and tasks.

Award-winning and epic poetry writer Robert Frost was famous for capturing the daily living of the commonplace people of his time. In the last verse of his classic poem "Two Tramps in Mud Time," we receive a glimpse into the ambiguity of marrying together the two halves of our lives through the example of the woodcutter's passion for his trade.

> But yield who will to their separation,
>
> My object in living is to unite
>
> My avocation and my vocation
>
> As my two eyes make one in sight.
>
> Only where love and need are one,
>
> And the work is play for mortal stakes,
>
> Is the deed ever really done
>
> For Heaven and the future's sakes.

You may want to spend quality time working out what your life description is by jotting down some areas you are responsible for in your family and personal life. If you have a job description from work, take it home and look at it more deeply and with different eyes. As you review your responsibilities, ask yourself, "How could I bring more compassionate purpose to this particular responsibility I have?" Save for a few areas that may not be applicable to this purpose, I know for sure you will discover more that are.

I would concur with Martin Luther King, Jr., when he summons, "If it falls your lot to be a street sweeper in life, sweep streets...like Beethoven composed music. Sweep streets...so well that all the hosts of heaven and earth will have to pause and say, "Here lived a great street sweeper who swept his job well."

A Father's Love

Peter shares with us his thoughts on how putting "skin in the game" has become a mantra of sorts for him. Although his vocation is a business manager, his avocation lies in his family, where he shares that he has learned compassion from his son. No one needs an MRI scan to know that our children are our best teachers on how to give and receive love. Peter says compassion, at its most intimate level, can only be defined as giving part of yourself in care or service to another. He then continues:

> If you provide "skin in the game" then you receive a vested return on investment, whether it is physical, emotional, or spiritual. When I reflect on this statement, I can only assume that we have a deeper purpose in life than simply being and living. If we had no emotional aspects to our brain, then we would breathe, consume food, live life, and eventually die. When we engage the emotional part of our life, we can and often do undertake a different existence.
>
> In the past 10 years, I have found a newly developed part of life, likely occurring in parallel with the birth of my only child, a son. I have found as a parent that I can take several paths in caring for this dependent individual. It began as a physical relationship—him needing food, clothing, warmth, diaper changes, etc. It has evolved into a purpose, brought on by a language-learning disability on his part. His condition is very mild, yet very important in a world that does not have

> any patience and/or limited flexibility for those that cannot keep up.
>
> I had thought early on that I really wanted a genius child, someone who could show me the way with their knowledge and skills, someone who would teach me by how they could adapt better when I gave him more opportunities than I had myself. In the end, he has taught me humility and caring—the compassion we talk about above. I have become compassionate because I have had to put "skin in the game" with my family. They need my time, my protection, my guidance, and my flexibility, as well as unconditional love. Giving of ourselves, of any of our talents, is exponentially enhanced when we can tie compassion into it, putting our own "skin into the game," and if we get that, we will be better for it.

To be purposeful is not something we choose to do one minute but not the next. It is a full-on commitment; it is as though one cannot do anything but put "skin in the game." It is joyfully non-optional because you would feel off balance if you made any other choice. And as Peter says, when we give of ourselves with compassion, we change the way we live and deepen the meaning of our lives

Beginner's Mind

The late Shunryu Suzuki, a Soto Zen monk who helped popularize Japanese Zen Buddhism in America, is also the author of the spiritual classic, *Zen Mind, Beginner's Mind,* which is a must-read for all students of meditation to assist them in avoiding the trappings of the intellectual mind.

Buddhists reference cultivating a beginner's mind to see past the mind chatter of barriers and biases that get in our way and stop us from learning new actions. To learn something new, such as the action of compassionate purpose, we have to let go of what no longer serves us to make room for new concepts.

The beginner's mind has no expectation that you will buy into anything new, nor change your beliefs to anything in particular. The sole motive of the beginner's mind is to ask you to put aside current beliefs and expectations and place them safely and temporarily into a box. This way, you can come back and pick them up after you have heard or seen something from a new perspective. There is no pressure to change your mind on any topic; only to have an open mind—a beginner's mind.

Once you listen to this new idea with suspended judgments then you can return to the box and pull out your old ideals like a coat and put them back on… that is, if they haven't changed at all with any new insights you may have gathered. This process greatly reduces the pressure to change.

Peter's abiding love for his son led the way for him. In Brenda's case, her calling to unlearn old ways and acquire new learning required her to have a beginner's mind for her own healing from cancer.

> Compassion came into my life when I was diagnosed with my third bout of cancer, and told I had about one year to live. Until that time, compassion was something I never considered for myself, or for others. Allowing the cancer to be my "wake-up call," I began to read books about spiritual love and compassion, and that is when I realized that what I needed more than anything was compassion and forgiveness to replace the years of anger, resentment, and pain I was carrying.
>
> Thus began my healing journey into compassionate forgiveness for myself and others, and this ultimately helped me to heal the cancer that was eating away at my body and my soul. Today, compassion is a natural outgrowth of the life I live, and I joyously extend compassion to all beings that cross my path, as I watch them soften and transform. Serving this way enriches my life and uplifts my spirit.

Brenda's story tells us that compassionate purpose comes to us disguised in different ways to show us our true compassionate selves. Due to her beginner's mind she was able to discard old paradigms that no longer served her.

A Mother's Gift

Brenda's story resonates with me at a personal level because it warmly welcomed me to recall my own mother's voyage with cancer. Two days before entering the hospital for the last time, she sat curled up with a blanket on my living room couch while I made dinner. As we chatted about nothing in particular, she stopped mid-sentence, looked up at me and, out of nowhere, quietly said, "You know, Olivia, in the end, there is only love."

These words were not typical language my mom would have used. She was someone who was not effusive; she showed her love in deeds more than words. The unexpectedness of her declaration made what she said even more profound for me—she gave me words that will never leave my side.

I would say that my mother offered me the gift of her compassion. Even as she was readying herself for death, she offered me words to remind me that we never really die—because love is eternal.

Chronic illness and the death of loved ones remind us of what is most important, of what we are really here for—because, truly, in the end, all the material wealth in the world means little. The only thing that matters is living a life of compassion and knowing that, in the end, there really is only love and there is no greater purpose.

A Wish for You

Cleaning the toilets at Mother Teresa's Home became a metaphor for me that people and work can be unpleasant and grim, and even stinky, and that this is a human condition we cannot deny. In the following weeks, I volunteered four more times to clean the latrines. I did so to remind myself that this work in India and this work of compassion should not be romanticized because, sometimes—many times—compassionate purpose can be just plain shitty.

My work reminded me that we are all one, all created equal, that we all eat, and we all have natural body fluids. I thanked that Sister before I went home for helping me to move beyond my own barriers and into understanding that compassion lay in all things, all around me, with every action I take or choose not to take to my detriment.

I am convinced that we have a "life" and we have a "purpose"—and these are not inevitably conjoined. Each is distinct and, should there be a synergy that joins them, then that is an added gift. I have known too many discouraged people feeling like they have missed the life-purpose boat—that it had sailed without them. I am convinced that they can discover that purpose if only they put their mind to creating a charged moment when they ask themselves, what might that purpose be? Do not look for it to appear as a cruise liner, opulent and large; instead, it may come disguised as a rubber dinghy, simple but reliable. Regardless, it is still of equal importance and contribution.

Leo Buscaglia, a favorite author of mine, reminds us that the majority of us will live "quiet, unheralded lives as we pass through this world. There will most likely be no ticker-tape parades for us, no monuments created in our honor. But that does not lessen our possible impact, for there are scores of people waiting for someone just like us to come along; people who will appreciate our compassion, our unique talents. Someone who will live a happier life merely because we took the time to share what we had to give. Too often we underestimate the power of a touch, a smile, a kind word, a listening ear, an honest compliment, or the smallest act of caring, all of which have a potential to turn a life around. It's overwhelming to consider the continuous opportunities there are to make our love felt."

And so it is if we want it to be. May there be a desire to marry your vocation with your avocation. May you explore the eternal possibilities of compassionate purpose during the whole of your life in this world.

Chapter 6

Compassionate Belonging

Do more than belong: participate. Do more than care: help.
Do more than believe: practice. Do more than be fair: be kind.
Do more than forgive: forget. Do more than dream: work.

William Arthur Ward

We are already one, but we imagine that we are not.
What we have to recover is our original unity.

Thomas Merton

"I am because of who we are" is a definition of the South African philosophy of Ubuntu. Retired Archbishop and social rights activist Desmond Tutu believes that Ubuntu is the very essence of what it is to be human:

> You can't be human all by yourself, and when you have this quality—Ubuntu—you are known for your generosity. We think of ourselves far too frequently as just individuals, separated from one another, whereas you are connected and what you do affects the whole World. When you do well, it spreads out; it is for the whole of humanity.

A doctor will tell you that the average person has about 10 pints of blood coursing through their veins. If we know this to be fact, does it matter what country we were born in, what language we speak, what color our skin is, or what our faith is?

We all get lonely; we all grieve for the loss of loved ones. We have cravings and crying spells. We are disappointed—and we get over it. We smile and we laugh. We need love and affection.

Archbishop Tutu is right. We are mutually dependent upon one another—not only to survive, but, even more importantly, to thrive. We need to belong.

What does it mean—to belong? For the vast majority of us, this would be a feeling of inclusiveness, of being loved and valued for who we are and accepted into a group of people. We relate belonging with words such as "connecting," "fitting in," "bonding," "companionship," "association," "kinship," or, as aboriginal cultures would say, "all my relations."

However we choose to define these connections, we are all kin either by blood or by common purpose; and, even when we don't believe we have anything in common with another, we do—because we have a heartbeat.

It is astonishing to me that we forget this simple fact—that we let so much divide and alienate us. We forget that our heartbeat infuses us all with the same physical and metaphysical qualities: it infuses our bodies with life force, our souls with love, our minds with hope, and all three of these with the need to belong.

A Basic Need

There is belonging, and then there is compassionate belonging. These are distinct in my view. Traditional belonging is experiencing connectedness through a recreational team, a school, a job, or a social or political group. All are imbued with a common purpose, but they may also generate a narrow sense of belonging.

Groups like these make up the fabric of our lives and keep everything in synergistic motion; we go merrily along our way, taking these relationships for granted, having an expectation that they will meet our immediate needs and wants.

Our connectedness to them varies. These are not relationships based on compassion—they are based on any number of other factors. Did my child get a passing grade? Was the snow plowed on my street? How can I get a promotion? Can our team make it to the finals? Who should I vote for?

As a matter of fact, we often use these groups and many others to feel a sense of belonging—and yet, unintentionally, exclude others by winning, by dominating, or by elimination.

In the world we live in today—with so much disunity and division—more than ever, we need to turn to one another with a renewed sense of collaboration and decrease the social disconnect and social injustice that currently surrounds us.

It is true. We are individual. We have dreams to pursue, goals to achieve, hopes to bring to reality. And yet we are also so much more than that when we join together in compassionate belonging, when we join hands and we move from one to oneness.

Ordinary People

Jerry shares a story that illustrates how these qualities play an active, if unrecognized, role in our lives.

> Ten years ago, I moved my family into a bigger city. Unsure of the decision that my wife and I made, we figured we had better opportunities in terms of our careers. At the time we moved we had two young children; one was a little over two years of age and our youngest was only one.

So far, this is a pretty ordinary story, isn't it? A young family setting out to establish itself takes a risk by moving to a new place. They are strangers in a new territory, but they are resilient and fueled by hope.

> Because I was doing shift work at the hospital as a lab technician, it was difficult for my wife to get a job. Daycare and renting an apartment were expensive, so we struggled and we learned financing in the hardest way possible. Pennies were accounted for and leisure time was very rare. The secondhand store became very popular for us and nothing could be wasted.
>
> My oldest child was four years old and started preschool when I decided to move to a private lab. The hours of work were better and we were able to manage our life and time. Three months after I started with my new job, a tragedy struck my family.
>
> My oldest son was diagnosed with leukemia, a debilitating disease that could kill him if not treated properly. To make the matter worse, my wife had a nervous breakdown the day we found out my son's illness.

In a flash, Jerry and his family were grappling with crises beyond the capability of their little ship, and yet Jerry was determined...

> I had to do what was needed. I spoke to my manager and told her what happened to my family and requested a leave of absence from my work to take care of them. She was very understanding of my situation and even offered her help.
>
> My son was started in his chemotherapy. Too young to receive radiation, the high dose of medication had made him totally weak, unable to walk, almost bedridden and he had to stay in the hospital....

> In the next three months, our little savings started to deplete while the bills kept piling up. I was so stressed out. I thought I was going to lose my mind.

From One to Oneness

In "Compassionate Purpose," I spoke of how there may come a time when we may be in need, when we may need to receive compassion, to receive care. In a city, without an extensive family network to support him, and at a new job, Jerry did not have a community to turn to.

> One day, I received a phone call from my work. The call was from the owner of the private lab I was working at. He said that he wanted to see me and to discuss some matters.
>
> After receiving the call, my heart started to beat faster; I was nervous and started panicking. I was sure that I would be losing my job....
>
> The day came to meet him. I knocked on his office door. As I stood there, I felt like running away to avoid meeting him...I was thinking of just quitting my job and maybe going onto social assistance until my son and my wife got better.
>
> Then the door opened and there, standing in front of me, was a bearded man, slightly chunkily built, with a very strong face. He let me in and asked me to take a seat. I sat quietly and felt totally intimidated.
>
> After a few seconds that felt like hours, he finally spoke. He said that he heard what happened to my family, particularly my son, and he felt really sorry. As soon as he

said those words, tears came down on my face. Here I was, sitting in front of a total stranger and crying. It must have been five minutes until I managed to control myself.

He handed me a box of tissues to wipe my tears away, then he spoke again. He said that, while I was away taking care of my family, all the staff had fundraised to help me. He said that, as a father of two young boys, he felt my pain and suffering. As he handed me the envelope, I started crying again. I was speechless and unable to utter a word.

Then he spoke again and said that I was not to worry about my job, it would be there when I decided to come back. Also, I shouldn't worry about the days I missed working as the company would pay my full salary....

He stood up and walked around his oversize office table and stood beside me, putting his hand on my shoulder, and then he said, "We will always be here for you. So, go and take care of your family. They need you."

As we were walking towards the main hallway of the lab, I saw many of my co-workers. Many of them I did not even know and some only looked familiar. But there was one thing they all had as I looked at them—a warm smile and sincerity, understanding, and profound compassion.

Many of them gave me hugs, some gave me assuring words, and some cried with me. Many gave me their gentle touch and reassuring smile. As I left I felt like a big boulder was lifted off my shoulder.

Jerry's story is not just about one man and his family, but about the creation of a circle of oneness—his colleagues joined together, hands clasped and united to lift him up.

The Common Good

When one of us is in pain we are all in pain. When one of us is hurting we are all hurting. When this circle of oneness is acted upon—and when compassionate belonging is rooted to the core of a group of individuals who think beyond themselves to a thread of common good—then miracles like Jerry's are poised and waiting to happen.

Charlie Chaplin wrote, directed, and starred in his first talking picture movie in 1940, called *The Great Dictator*. He wrote these compelling lines, "Our knowledge has made us cynical; our cleverness, hard and unkind. We think too much and feel too little. More than machinery, we need humanity. More than cleverness, we need kindness and gentleness."

Whether the setting is home or work, Chaplin suggests that the methodologies we have applied in the past can no longer serve us as effectively as kindness and compassion can.

The Positive Tickets program described in 'Compassionate Optimism" attests to the truth of this assertion. What Superintendent Clapham had offered the kids he encountered was not just hope; it was also inclusion. It was recognition of who they were—bringing them into the circle of kindness, not exiling them to the outskirts.

Joan, a self-employed hairstylist, had medical coverage, but would have no paid sick leave for the six weeks' leave she required following an emergency surgery.

Her colleagues knew this would be a financial hardship for her, and so, without a word to Joan, they banded together to cut, color, perm, and style all of Joan's regular clients. On the day she returned to work, they presented her with a check for each service rendered so there was no lapse in her income.

When asked why they had done it, the answer was obvious. "Because," they said, "she would have done this for any one of us; we're a family."

John is another example of how oneness can change lives. John is a civic employee in the city where he lives. When he ran out of paid sick days and short-term disability for an unexpected illness, his colleagues took up a collection and sent it around. Except they were not collecting cash; instead, they asked for donations of unused sick days in increments over four hours to multiple days and then replenished his benefits account. Altogether, his comrades collected enough for him to take an additional two months off with pay—one heartfelt sick day at a time.

I am of the same mind as American singer-songwriter Tracy Chapman, who, in her poetic song, "Heaven Here On Earth," has lyrics that say it all: "I've seen and met angels wearing the disguise of ordinary people living ordinary lives."

Compassionate Civic Leadership

Compassionate belonging embraces individuals, creates community, and encompasses leadership from town to nation. Civic leadership is an especially potential-filled and influential circle for compassionate belonging by its natural connection to community.

One such example is Louisville, home of the Kentucky Derby—the "most exciting two minutes in sports"—which has run consecutively since 1875. The Derby draws crowds from around the world for two weeks of celebration and racing. They are also visiting a metropolis that is on a ten-year campaign to become a world-class compassionate city.

In 2011, Greg Fischer was sworn in as Mayor of Louisville, Kentucky, with an unusual election platform. It consisted of three promises to his city: health, education, and compassion.

While seated next to the Mayor during a luncheon in his beautiful and welcoming city, I asked him what advice he had for other civic leaders to accomplish something similar in their cities. His reply was both simple and profound. He said that you have to be willing to take a risk and stand for what you believe in, even when others may not.

Here was a politician who had been told by his campaign managers that compassion was not a platform to get elected on. Yet, there he was, elected Mayor, and with the backing of his city council, he had a strong agenda to move forward with his strategic plan and keystone: that "compassion is a common ground and unifying force in our polarized world."

The Mayor's Chief of Community Building, Sadiqa Reynolds, notes that their goal is not to "prescribe what compassionate acts people take, but to serve as a convenor of ideas and a facilitator." As just one example of their direction, "Give a Day" volunteer week was launched—citizens were asked to give one day of service to others as part of the Kentucky Derby Festival. The inaugural event netted over 90,000 acts of compassionate service. The goal is to make Give a Day part of the annual fabric of the city.

Reynolds sums it up succinctly by saying that having compassion "in your mind as you go about your work automatically begins to shift the way you craft your policy." Mayor Fischer has set out to make a difference and has successfully begun to embed it within the fiber of this city's government by not asking the traditional question of what can Louisville do to be compassionate, but, rather, "what does compassion want for Louisville?" and then seeking the answer from its citizens.

Weaving compassion into the Louisville community is accomplished through arts and culture, the civic involvement of local business, the use of restorative justice programs in the courts, and through education—with Spalding University becoming the first university to affirm the Charter for Compassion and declare that it has become a compassionate university.

This is one example of a city working to entwine compassion into its civic duties, while, across the globe, cities are affirming their desire to pursue compassion through the internationally recognized Compassionate Action Network International, with a mission to "grow and support a global movement of compassion" and to promote compassionate initiatives in "cities and regions, universities and schools, service groups, and other places where human beings gather."

Competitive Altruism

The city of Seattle, Washington, has been putting forth a challenge to other cities that want to expand their compassion into "competitive altruism" as Jon Ramer, Founder of the Compassion Games: Survival of the Kindest, refers to a brand of compassion with a warm twist of competition.

Jon tells me that competitiveness is "wired into our brains, so let's not pretend it's not there." Rather, let us make use of it to spread compassionate acts. Recently, Louisville and Seattle went head-to-head to see who could garner the most compassionate acts in a limited time frame—games that netted over 200,000 acts of compassion between the cities. Activities and projects are passionately driven through business, education, sports, civic leaders, and faith-based groups that step up to the healthy competition with zeal.

Where We Gather

It is within anyone's means to explore compassionate involvement at the municipal level. One does not have to be mayor; indeed, one must answer to an even higher calling—that of compassionate citizen.

Here is the question: Where are we as citizens? We all have a sense of the wellness of our neighborhoods, our towns, our cities. We know there are policies, protocols, and governance criteria in place to address issues and problems, and perhaps we rely on them. We remain passive citizens when we don't take action, even though we know we can be part of the solutions.

How can we engage and create inclusiveness where it is needed? How can we create belonging between youth and seniors, between schools and business?

If we think in terms of "where human beings gather," compassion has the potential to multiply far beyond the mere numbers gathered. By building trust, fostering interconnectedness, and cultivating inclusion, we can create cities where compassion is the sustainable energy lighting our neighborhoods.

Compassionate Youth

Free The Children, an international charity organization, is passionate about youth, volunteerism, and kids' potential to be the change they want to see in the world. We Act is a year-long school program that encourages youth to participate in a curriculum-based program to promote compassionate acts locally and to reach out globally. Here is a charity that has built strong foundations on "the understanding that by awakening the spirit of volunteerism in young people, anything is possible—injustices can be stopped, our local and global communities can be transformed for the better, and hope for the future can be sustained."

Last summer, at age 18, Sydney experienced awakening the "spirit of volunteerism" when she took up the call for a month with a tribe in Kenya with Free The Children.

> We associate connectedness with Facebook, Twitter, Instagram, and basically anything that prevents true connection. I joined 28 other students for this trip and I felt part of something bigger than myself. I took one of my mom's scarves so I was reminded of my own tribe as I excitedly explored this new one. The community with the Mamas—Masai women—was one where you never felt alone. There was always someone near, helping, doing, talking, singing, and moving things forward. The idea of "belonging" was all around me.
>
> No one passed by without saying Jambo, which is "hello" in Swahili, or to talk or to listen. The togetherness amidst these strangers was more than I felt back home. We learned to use their weapons, walked miles for water every day, dug a quarry for a new hospital, picked rocks, went on safari, played with local children, were taught to bead by the tribe's women—it was a tribe, a society, and community. It was what I was looking for here in North America and couldn't find it.
>
> On my trip back home I was aware that I was alone with so many people around. Facebook seemed futile.
>
> We in North America are so alone and lonely. People aren't friendly, they don't smile, and they don't help each other unless it's a crisis. There are pockets of communities here and there, but we are not made up of community. In my Kenyan tribe, belonging and gentle community just "was"... it wasn't created for you, done for you in a

> phony "'cause your visiting" way. It was just in the air, every single day.
> Belonging isn't created for anyone—it just exists for itself.

We Day

Sydney's passion for volunteerism began when she attended We Day in her hometown. Participating schools of We Act are invited to attend, packing thousands of energy-charged kids into stadiums full of entertainers, musicians, and inspirational leaders whose rally cry fosters interconnectedness, rouses volunteerism, and challenges youth to put compassion into action as active global citizens.

Craig and Marc Kielburger, founders of Free The Children, explain how We Day "represents the beginning of a lifetime of compassionate action. A study of We Day alumni from the past five years by Chicago-based research firm Mission Measurement found that 80 percent continued to volunteer an average of 150 hours last year, 83 percent donated to a non-profit or charity, and 78 percent of voting-age alumni voted in the most recent federal election—double the rate of their peers."

Connection and compassion create a sense of citizen ownership and belonging that is true, tangible community at its best.

Community in the Digital Age

Free The Children and We Day have used social technology to reach out to an entire generation of youth and link them across the globe. Here we have a bright generation of critical thinkers who do not see the digital world as separate from—but as an appendage or natural extension of—who they are.

How we feel about our surrounding community is dictated by the social interactions and connections we have established within our community. We find soul mates online, graduate from university, attend conferences, raise money for charities, join meet-up groups, connect with family and friends, share our travels, and diarize our lives for the world to see. Authors use it to reach out to their audience; I received responses from Hong Kong to Panama when I put out a request for contributors to this book.

The past decade has seen a shift to increased global access, fast-paced mobility, and a thrust forward and backward in how we communicate through the medium of technology. Here we have another dichotomy as discussed in "A Science": while we aim for a sense of belonging brought together by the disintegration of borders—where time is anytime, anywhere—and where a passport to enter the digital world does not require being fingerprinted, it also simultaneously creates separation as we surrender our part of our interpersonal ability to communicate. Emoticons cannot embrace you with a loving hug, look into your eyes, or give you the warmth of a smile.

Technology has forever changed our global classroom and global community. We cannot yet predict what will happen between relationships and technology and how they will find a cozy place together in the future. What we do know is that, as one door closes slightly, another is left open. We have found a new way to reach out to each other, and hopefully create the vital bonding as a community we all desire.

A Key Ingredient

Thinking in terms of what compassion would do has also been making its way into commerce. Rod Brooks is someone who has a passion for marketing messages, and when not working as the VP of Marketing for a larger Washington insurance company, you will find him speaking at conferences. Rod shares his views on how marketing and compassion fit together.

> Where social engagement has flourished and virtual communities have formed in newly familiar places like Face-

> book, Twitter, and YouTube, compassion and empathy have become important communication planks in the implementation of social marketing strategy. Marketers are remembering the required fundamentals for making sustainable human connections—selfless, inspiring, and compassionate acts that connect brands with consumers. Marketing messages from relationship-driven companies—content that reflects human characteristics—will be more fully and effectively received, understood, valued, utilized, and shared.

If we have a desire to move compassion forward in all aspects of our lives, then using our purchasing power to support relationship-driven companies with global caring values can only benefit us all. It is a way of practicing the cycle of reciprocity as discussed in "A Devotion." We need to consider how our values align with the products we purchase. Buying items that are created by child labor, that are not fairly traded, or have a detrimental environmental impact would be contrary to the value of compassion.

The Ones We Walk By

Sydney mentioned the disconnect that can occur within social media. Rod shared how marketers need to make the links between products and buyers with real human connections. Asking "What would compassion do?" in any given situation is a pointed way to take affirmative action. Whether living in a rural town, or an urban sprawl, there are bountiful opportunities—and it likely means stepping into the unidentified for some of us.

In my case, the unknown was not a natural endeavor. My story goes back three years when a few members of my family decided to forego traditional Christmas presents for the adults and place the money into a common pile with each taking an equal portion. The aim was to go do something good for someone else within the year.

My aspiration was to make friends with someone homeless; I just wasn't sure how to do it. I recognize this sounds rather lame—and to write it down it looks even more awkward. However, I plead guilty.

For me, this was a challenge, and one I had struggled against for years living in a large urban city and walking by many disenfranchised in my own neighborhoods as well as throughout my travels abroad. Do I give money? Do I buy food? Should I strike up a conversation? What would I say and how should I say it? Do I ignore them or avoid eye contact? Then, perhaps, they won't ask me for anything, and then I don't have to decide to whom to give or not give that day.

To Each Our Own Corner

It has distressed me for years that I had, in so many ways, formed opinions that needed to be discarded—or judgments that were erroneous—against many of my neighbors. The homeless are my neighbors: they lived somewhere in my community, picked up refundable bottles in my community, panhandled for work on my community sidewalks, walked in the same rain and snow and enjoyed the same sun in my community, and used their money to buy what they could in my community stores.

Indeed, my community is their community; we all breathe the same air, drink the same water, and walk the same streets. One part of me wants to say, "Go find work," and another part of me wants to feed them a hearty dinner and help them write a resume.

I suspect much of my discomfort is because I don't know what to say or how to repair what seems irreparable much of the time. I wonder if we can actually be paralyzed with too much compassion and embarrassed because we are "haves" while others "have not." As someone who speaks profes-

> You cannot belong to anyone else, until you belong to yourself.
>
> Pearl Bailey

sionally for a living, it seems odd to me that I am short on words when I walk by the man, the woman, my homeless neighbors on the street—and yet, I am.

For certain, I give money again and again; buy something to eat or drink from time to time; and I always smile, because I am good at smiling. I say, "Good morning," or, "Hi," or some nicety, or, "Sorry, not today," when the request comes for one too many handouts in a day.

Yes, without fail, I am always pleasant, and I have spent many Christmases and Thanksgivings serving meals to the homeless in local missions—doing the best I can and loving every moment of those group connections. But I know it is, by no means, sufficient for what seems an endless problem.

For the most part, I try to do the right thing even though, many times, I may struggle with a feeling of being disconnected. I believe this detachment was partly because of the sheer lack of meaningful conversation with these neighbors of mine who hold claim to their working corner—not unlike I lay claim to my work.

Truth be told, I felt intimidated, nervous, and unsure of what to say or do because of my false perception and my barriers of fear that stopped my ability to experience the deeper sense of belonging that I so wanted to achieve. Would they reject me if I tried to say anything past my few niceties?

Would they lash out in anger at me or with contempt, or just plain ignore me?

My Christmas Wish

It is interesting what your mind will contrive when you do not feel at ease with something or someone—making the tales we weave even more dramatic. With my Christmas wish guiding me forward to move past these barriers that I solely owned, I aimed to get to know a neighbor gentleman whose corner work station was the local drugstore.

He would read his tattered paperback books perched alongside everything he owned so neatly bundled in his organized backpack. Late one afternoon I announced to myself, "Today is the day," so I headed to the drugstore, courage in hand, to buy something I didn't really need just so I could have an opportunity to strike up a conversation.

"How is your day going?" I asked politely.

"I am having a marvelous day! How about you?" he replied.

So I ventured onward. "What novel are you reading? The cover looks interesting."

"Oh, it's a really good mystery novel," my neighbor told me, along with the title.

"Now that's an attention-grabber. Are the characters as interesting?"

His eyes lit up as he took me into the storyline, explaining each character's personality and the antagonist and protagonist roles they each took in the novel.

"Great to meet a fellow reader! My name is Olivia, but some of my friends call me Liv," I said, smiling.

My Neighbor

My neighbor, whose name is Don, likes to read mystery novels. From that day forward we had a link of sorts between two strangers—one asking for a hand up, one asking how to stickhandle the unknown, both wanting the same connection.

Over the next few months, every time I saw Don we would talk about books as a common bond. Don never asked me for anything, and every few weeks I would ask him what he might need inside the store and would pick him up some sundries.

Knowing I needed to use my Christmas wish money, I made a suggestion to Don that I would like to get him something that he could use—like some clothes, a haircut, groceries; it was his choice, and I asked him to think about it and let me know next time I saw him. Interestingly, a few weeks later, he suggested a small gift card from the drugstore so he could pick up a few things he needed. A great idea, and I walked in to purchase the card.

So there I was, with Christmas dollars' worth of wishes and saying to myself, "You can't give him all these cards. What if he sells them for alcohol or drugs or cigarettes? What if...or what about what if...or what about my about what if...?"

Part of me wanted to trust him to use them wisely; part of me wanted to put conditions on what he could buy with them; part of me thought I should dole them out in $25 increments. I stopped midway down the toothpaste aisle with thoughts swimming in my head once again: "Olivia, stop right here. You are judging him and believing that you think you know better than he does for himself. What's the point of giving something if it's done with conditions, expectations, and judgments?"

So I bought one big card, some little treats, and socks to go in the bag, and unconditionally handed it over to Don to do with them whatever he felt was perfect for him. Then I let it go. Don was shocked at the amount, as he had been expecting a $10 card, he said.

Over the coming months our friendship continued. We chatted. We would tell each other what was going on in our lives in sound bites. One day, Don said he no longer wanted to live on the street. He'd had enough and was now renting a couch and had access to clean clothes, took a daily bath, and cooked his own food. "Now I can look for work," he proudly informed me.

My Friend

One day we talked for a long time about the changes he had made in the past year, when out of nowhere, he said, "I want you to know that I never used those gift cards for anything but good stuff in the store. I wouldn't even buy smokes with them because I felt that this wouldn't have been right to use them this way when they were a gift."

I had never suggested what he could or could not do with the cards. Nor did I ever ask him what he did with them. But Don offered this information up to me.

It was a lesson for me about truly trusting the wisdom of others, and he had just taught me that true compassion comes from the heart—unconditionally and without judgments.

Don picked his own life up and trusted his own wisdom when the time was right and he was ready. I so wanted to hug him to celebrate his success, but alas, I stopped myself once again because I didn't want to intrude on his space or make him feel uncomfortable.

Yet again my new friend was my teacher and as I walked away, he called out to me, "Hey, Liv, would you mind if I gave you a big hug? It would mean a lot to me." In that moment I agreed completely with author Antoine de Saint-Exupéry, who had commented that compassion "that does not take its object in its arms" has no value.

That hug with Don has become one of my most memorable hugs ever.

We are All One—Even in Trauma

We are so wonderfully interdependent upon one another. I do believe we need each other to walk one another home. Without Don's embrace of friendship and display of his authentic self, I suspect it would have taken me many more years—if it ever happened—to move so gracefully out of my own barriers and fears toward understanding one to oneness.

Sylvia, now 71 years young, stills works in her life calling and tells me compassion is "having no enemies within or without" and "it

> If you really want to make a friend, go to someone's house and eat with him... the people who give you their food give you their heart.
>
> Cesar Chavez

springs from the heart that knows its own darkness because it has looked inside." Hers is a concrete knowing about our interconnectedness because Sylvia speaks from her experience in trauma, suicide bereavement, and loss and grief counseling:

> The suffering and the courage of people of all walks of life have touched my heart and soul in ways that shape me into the person I am today. Many people do service for those in need and may have the skills of empathy yet may not have compassion.
>
> Compassion has to do with a deep knowing of our interconnectedness with all beings. I mean recognition that the children's cries and the stress of the polar bear and the predator down the street are not separate from me or from one another. At some level I am the child, the polar bear, and the predator.
>
> Separation is an illusion. We are all hurting in this game of separation. When I can open my heart and smile, I can be with the other, free of judgment or attachment.

We must get out of our own way—a true sense of belonging cannot exist with all the negative debris we strew in our midst. Monique's belief that compassionate belonging is "respectfully helping others as equals, while never applying judgment" stood out for me.

> My goal is to become spontaneously compassionate, to recognize and react, to give freely without being motivated by the thought of rewarding consequences or weighing what the emotional investment might be.
>
> I am a long way from this goal: my friend has been arrested for a most heinous crime. He lives in isolation and needs social contact. I feel repulsed by his actions and I am struggling to see beyond his crime.

While Monique challenges herself to get "beyond the crime," most of us are just struggling to get beyond the day-to-day judgments of everyday life issues.

Who among us has not struggled with disparaging voices in our head? I, for one, can barely get through a day without reproachful thoughts—some fleeting while others lend themselves to ruminations—all passing through my consciousness like a constant tide sweeping up against the cluttered shoreline.

I do not have an answer for Monique. I can only hope that I may show the same self-awareness and strength in the face of challenges to my compassion.

We are All One—Even in War

Sharon Henderson and Yuri Dojc have created an immeasurably thoughtful book, aptly named *Honour,* which gives tribute to World War II veterans. Henderson tells me that "compassion can be giving someone a voice so that a greater understanding of life experiences, especially those as complex as war, can be shared."

Sharon recounts the story of Dr. Eldon Comfort. When he enlisted in the army, he believed the enemy to be "so evil that the end justified the means."

> "I quickly realized that the enemy was, in fact, Hitler and those who did his bidding; but that was not the soldiers on the German front line," he explains. "I came to believe that there must be a better way."
>
> As a Lieutenant with the 2nd Divisional Army, he oversaw a section of radio telephone and dispatch offices that were responsible for directing gunfire on the front lines. "You realize the gravity of your responsibilities quickly," he adds.
>
> As the Allies began planning for their final thrust in 1945, Eldon was asked to design a signal diagram for the advance. It involved heavy artillery and thousands of guns to soften the area for the troops' advance. "I've never stopped thinking how many were killed in those positions," he softly recalls.
>
> Eldon's disillusionment would propel him to become a peace activist, his influence on the movement recognized in 2001 when he was given an Honourary Doctor of Sacred Letters.

Despite his experiences, Dr. Comfort was able to move from judgment to recognition that we are all interconnected, and that what happens to one happens to us all.

What Would Compassion Do?

We are all citizens from somewhere, with one or more of these versions of relationship connectors slotted into our bloodstream like a living organism creating a longing to take us away from separation and loneliness. Aristotle knew this only too well, declaring that friends were the glue that bound cities together. Novelist and social humanist Kurt Vonnegut suggested that young people today should do many things with their lives, but the most daring thing they could do would be to "create stable communities in which the terrible disease of loneliness can be cured."

Loneliness and isolation are factors everyone experiences to some degree in one's life—whether situational until they eventually pass, or, sadly, they become a part of one's daily routine. The US census suggests that, as of 2010, 31 million people live alone, which is up from 18 million only 25 years ago. There is a growing body of research indicating that how we live today is creating an epidemic of loneliness.

Shelley wrote to me about a time in her life when she could have experienced great loneliness and isolation and instead discovered what a community can do when bonded by compassion. Her brother-in-law was dying of cancer. The teachers she worked with remembered...

> ...the names of my nephews who were soon to be fatherless. They remembered about the treatments that were being performed and the hospital stays.
>
> Oh, and the outpouring of support for a fundraiser that was held. I can't even describe how much compassion was shown there. So many people came that there was not enough room to seat everyone.
>
> I thought people would be upset about not getting their meal but they were happy for us that we had such a great turnout! Can you imagine? I still tear up when I think about it. There were so many teachers that I barely knew who donated money or came to the dinner out of compassion for us.
>
> What hit home for me was that I don't think I ever had shown true compassion for a co-worker that I was not close to. Not in such a deep, unhurried, and totally giving way.

I so valued Shelley's personal observation that we have a tendency to give compassion more readily to people we know. If any of us were to go to any work or social event or walk down the street, we would bump into strangers, co-workers, or acquaintances we aren't close to; the opportunity would be there for us to do our part to create a sense of belonging. The opportunity would be there to connect with others in a deeply meaningful way.

If we feel unsure, we need only ask ourselves, "What would compassion do?"

Sometimes the gap we may be aware of in our lives is a gentle reminder to pause, reflect, and realize that we may be lacking connection and community, and that we need to commit to getting some of that nourishment into our lives once again. Here are some thoughts on how to answer the question, "What would compassion do?"—how to bridge that gap:

Create a new circle of friendship
- Meet someone from another generation
- Talk to a neighbor
- Create or join a compassion club

Reach beyond your current boundaries
- Identify what makes you feel included and forward that to someone else
- Volunteer in your community
- Commit to a conscious act of kindness every week

Ensure everyone feels valued, respected, and heard
- Acknowledge someone you usually ignore
- Ask, "What do you think?"
- Listen with love

Family Tapestry

Many places offer us opportunities to create community and connection, whether they are through volunteer service or work. My sister Anna is employed in an assisted living seniors' home and loves her vocation of service to the residents. Anna values the timeless stories of experiences they have had throughout their lives and ones they willingly share with her.

She lights up as she shares their accomplishments as though they were her own relatives and has told me more than once that for her, it is like having a multitude of grandmas and grandpas. Anna wrote me that compassion, to her, means giving as much of herself as is required to help another person, and shares some insights from a generational perspective. She says:

> When I took my job at a seniors' home, I hadn't realized just how much compassion I would be required to give, or how wonderful it would feel to give it. Being of a younger generation, I had, in my own mind, glorified the golden years. I was aware of the health issues that come with getting older, but had never considered all the other range of things they have to deal with.
>
> Missing a husband or wife that they lost 10 years past, or a child, financial problems, depression, loss of memory,

> and the list goes on—and it is not glorious. Once we open our eyes and our hearts to what others feel, we then realize we are all the same.
>
> This job has given me more compassion than I knew I had to give. Compassion is such a natural thing that we already have within ourselves to give and it never gets exhausting, because compassion replenishes itself as it's used. One of the best parts of the human condition is that, the more we understand that we are all human, that we all have the same needs and sufferings, the easier it becomes to feel compassion with anyone who needs it.

For these wise elders, this is their newfound community. They come together with strangers at first and create a new sense of belonging—all dealing with the same human condition. We are that elder in the seniors' home. One day that will be us, regardless of how young and vital we feel in this moment.

Let me finish with one more story. Darlene was too weak to attend the most precious day of a parent's life—her child's wedding. The chemotherapy had taken its toll on her health and she had resigned herself to missing this special day, breaking down in tears every time it was mentioned.

To the staff and doctors on Ward 6200 this was not acceptable, so they hatched a plan to mastermind a wedding day by coordinating a live video stream into her hospital room from the church where the ceremony was being performed. Placed by her bedside was a handmade corsage and her freshly pressed mother-of-the-bride dress. Her dull hospital room was now decorated. Darlene's hair and makeup was done to perfection by the staff.

A community was created, a family was connected, and a woman was surrounded and embraced with love by the unit staff and doctors that day.

We may believe that we are all different, but we all belong to a larger universal clan. As we weave in and out of our immediate families, workgroups, and local communities, so we create a tapestry invisible to the eye, but not the heart.

In *A Christmas Carol*, the ghost of Marley is burdened by a long and heavy chain he had forged during his life—each link representing some way in which he had cut himself off from his fellows by unkind acts or greed.

I like to think we have the power to weave a tapestry in our lives. It may be colorful, well-kept, and honored or it may be tattered and neglected. The pattern and strength arise from how attentive we are to the choices we make. Every day, we add more to it. Weave well, so your tapestry reflects the unique and loving contribution only you can make.

Chapter 7

Compassionate Presence

*Empathy is full of presence to what's alive
in the other person at this moment.*

John Cunningham

A good heart is better than all the heads in the world.

Edward Bulwer-Lytton

Bob is a volunteer with seniors and became a friend to a resident who had endured World War II. Bob believed his friend's memories needed to be set down. So, once a week, he travelled to the assisted living home, listened, taped, and then returned home to transcribe his friend's stories.

Bob is blind and has been losing his vision for 20 years. In an interview, he told me that 45 minutes of recording would take him about 10 hours to transcribe, but that didn't matter because he knew he had time and his friend, who was in his late 90s and declining, did not.

65,000 words, 140 pages, and 30 audiotapes. That, and 3 bus connections, took Bob to the assisted living home and his friend.

There are people who cross our paths whose presence is felt long after they have left the space they occupied. Our time with them may have been as brief as Sudan's encounter with two children in "A Science," or as lengthy as Edie's four-year embrace of Beth in "Compassionate Purpose," and yet, their presence will linger.

In the stories we've shared, we've met someone who, by their compassionate presence, brought so much else—relief, laughter, acceptance, companionship. The list is too short to encompass the resonance compassionate presence leaves in its wake.

> Courage is what it takes to stand up and speak; courage is also what it takes to sit down and listen.
>
> Winston Churchill

When they first met, Bob's friend was "rather cantankerous"—he suffered from loneliness and isolation, and at times, anxiety. Bob and his beloved guide dog, Dusty, alleviated his suffering during their visits. After his friend passed away, Bob continued transcribing the memoirs so he could gift them to his friend's family.

I asked Bob what he had taken away from his experience, and he replied that he thought, "all humans seek and receive three personal treasures in their lives, namely, respect, appreciation, and love."

Presence is Twofold

Compassionate presence is twofold. It is holding firmly to an unhindered commitment to being present to oneself. It is holding a sacred space for another: *you are important and I am here for you.*

An unhindered commitment to being present to oneself. It sounds selfish, and yet it is not. We cannot really be present for someone else when we are absent with ourselves. We see this absenteeism in the news every day when someone who offers much to the public world is suddenly revealed to have a troubled private life. *How can that be?* we wonder. *How can such a gulf exist?*

We also see it when someone lives in a state of constant agitation, as though she is a small boat on a storm-tossed sea, always in danger of capsizing.

There are others who seem to have a different way about them. They seem to hold a center, a calmness and optimism. Storm clouds may brew, and yet they hold fast the tiller and steer a steady course.

We may regard them and ask ourselves, "How can we make our own way with such compassion and presence?"

Let me answer by asking you a simple yet profound question, "How aware are you of yourself at this very moment?"

I would invite you to spend a little time with your answer. I would invite you to notice the most basic things. Whether you are seated on a chair or a couch, whether your body feels at rest, whether you are alone or with others, whether there is sound in the background or quiet. I would offer that you simply take a breath and be, no matter where you are. Feel that breath travel into your body and feel your body receive it.

If you notice how crowded you feel by things that call your attention, perhaps you could imagine setting each of these pieces in something, or on something, that is capable of holding them safely for you.

In "A Devotion," I spoke of time to be contemplative, of finding your true north. Once you have done so here, imagine a warmth that surrounds and protects you as you go about your day; a warmth that comforts and nurtures.

That warm energy is the calm and strength, the wellspring of compassion that lives within us, ready to sustain us whenever we allow ourselves a little time to ask, "Where am I in all of this?"

Bob's blindness came on while he was a high school science teacher, a vocation he loved. He continued to teach, but no longer does so. Now he brings his love of science and enquiry to his volunteer work, holding discussions on nanotechnology, the 2012 Mayan calendar, or stem cell research with seniors at the assisted living home. When I spoke with Bob, I had the impression of someone who was positive, centered, and calm, with a great sense of humor. I had the impression of someone whose hand was steady at the helm, no matter what the storm.

By holding a sacred space for ourselves, we allow ourselves to be present with others.

Compassionate Presence for Self

Norma has been a mental health and addictions counselor for over 27 years. Her work epitomizes the twofold nature of compassionate presence: holding a compassionate space for herself while offering the same for another.

> I have learned so much about compassion, for on a daily basis, I sit and listen to stories of pain and struggle as well as extreme courage. When I am connected to my heart and it has not been hardened by these many stories, I easily show compassion. When I take on too much—or, should I say, take less time for self—I feel disconnected from my heart and find it hard to be compassionate.

In this most difficult chapter, I speak to the hard stuff that may arise from one's desire to live and act with compassion. There is a voice that must speak to the practice one must devote to living with compassionate presence for oneself and others. There is a voice that must speak to the potential frailty and weariness that may ensue when we are immersed in situations that challenge our equilibrium.

This weariness, which comes in varying degrees of strength and duration, can affect those in a "helping" line of work. It can apply to volunteers, human resource workers, counselors, teachers, aid workers, insurance and claims adjusters, and non-profit workers. It can apply to family and friends acting as caregivers or those who are reaching a hand out to the disenfranchised, whether locally or globally.

I believe we are kind by nature; we do not want to see any living thing in pain and suffering. But helping our fellow human beings is not trouble free. The closer one is to a constant barrage of distress—either working with it daily or witnessing it—the more susceptible one becomes to exhaustion. The exposure encourages the psyche's desire to save itself from harm's way. There is a progressive erosion of one's ability to demonstrate compassion. In effect, we suffer compassion fatigue. We risk losing the very treasures that Bob revealed we seek.

While in Morocco, I volunteered at an orphanage and spent three weeks in the nursery caring for abandoned newborn babies. The children suffered from malnutrition, poverty, and a lack of emotional support and physical touch. The overworked caregivers had the heart—just not the resources. For months after returning home, I would wake up to the sounds of a baby crying. My experience gave me so much respect for those who are in the front line of compassionate care on a daily basis.

As we make our way together through this chapter, may you recognize that your self-care is worthy of practice and devotion. May you regain your true north, restore your optimism, and revive your compassionate presence.

Ordinary Heroes

Debra had been married for 24 years and had 2 children aged 11 and 16 when her husband was diagnosed with a rare incurable disease.

> After seeing 27 specialists in 7 hospitals in 3 cities in 2 years, my husband transitioned from living at home to living in a nursing home 18 months ago. The last 4 years have been about pursuing a diagnosis; navigating the healthcare system; caring for him as the slow march of degeneration took away his ability to drive, then walk, to talk coherently, and... be who he was. Within the anticipatory loss, the many changing levels of "new normal" a life-limiting disease brings—while trying to keep up the facade of managing it all: 2 kids, 4 pets, career, and home—I lost myself.

Jody Picoult is a bestselling author. In her 2003 mystery book, *Second Glance,* she shares insight into the heroes in our lives. "Heroes," she tells us, "didn't leap tall buildings or stop bullets with an outstretched hand; they didn't wear boots and capes. They bled, and they bruised, and their superpowers were as simple as listening, or loving. Heroes were ordinary people who knew that even if their own lives were impossibly knotted, they could untangle someone else's. And maybe that one act could lead someone to rescue you right back."

We are all "ordinary people"—brave women and men doing heroic acts of kindness and compassion in the simplest of ways. We show up, even on those days when we feel like we can't listen or have nothing more to give. Every one of us—at some point—needs to be rescued.

Too Stressed to Be Present

According to the American Psychological Association, a recent survey indicates that 54 percent of Americans say they are concerned about the amount of stress in their lives and 80 percent state that the economy is a significant cause of stress.

Nearly one-quarter of Canadians report that most days are extremely or quite stressful. The daily stress rating is highest between the ages of 35 and 54 years of age. No one will dispute that the more that stress consumes our life force, the less endurance we have for delivering compassionate care to ourselves and others. The argument being that there is only so much time to go around, and if a caregiver's priority is to give it away to others, the caregiver is left depleted and without enough reserve for self. Being without this precious reserve to protect ourselves may leave us vulnerable to potentially unhealthy ways of being.

Here is a story I like to share as a reminder of how easy it can be to lose one's way when too many internal and external pressures are pushed up against us. Interestingly, we rarely even see we have been meandering down an unhealthy path until, alas, we are too far down the road and a kind friend reminds us—or, in this case, a mother's love.

> Rachel was visiting her mother and told her that she had too much going on between her work and her home life. She confessed that she was becoming so discouraged, she wanted to give up—she was tired of struggling. As soon as she resolved one problem, a new one seemed to arise.
>
> Her mother ushered Rachel to the kitchen, filled three pots of water, and placed each on a very hot flame. Soon the pots came to a boil. In the first, she dropped six carrots; in the second, she placed two eggs; and, into the last, she poured ground coffee beans. She let all three pots sit and boil, without saying a word.

> After fifteen minutes, she turned off the burners, lifted out the carrots, and placed them in a bowl. She spooned out the eggs and placed them on a plate. Then she ladled up the coffee and placed it in a cup. Turning to Rachel, she asked, "Tell me, what do you see?" "Carrots, eggs, and coffee," Rachel replied, a bit confused. "What does it mean, Mother? What are you trying to tell me?" Rachel asked.
>
> Her mother explained that each of these objects had been boiled in water, and each had reacted differently. The carrots—originally strong and hard—had emerged weak and soft. The egg had been fragile, but as its thin outer shell had protected its liquid interior, it sat in the boiling water until its insides became hardened. The ground coffee beans, on the other hand, had converted the boiling water to coffee.
>
> "Which are you?" she asked her daughter. "When adversity knocks on your door, how do you respond? Are you a carrot, an egg, or a coffee bean? The bean actually changes that which would cause it pain as the water gets hot; the bean releases fragrance and flavor. If you are like the bean, then when things are at their worst, you get better and change the situation around you. When the hour is dark and trials are great, elevate yourself to another level."

Have we not all been a carrot, an egg, or a coffee bean throughout our lives? I know I certainly have.

Are you the carrot that seems strong, but with pain and adversity, wilts, becomes soft, and loses its strength? Sometimes I have thrown my hands up in the air in apathy and admitted defeat.

Are you the egg that starts with a malleable heart, but changes with the heat? Did you have a soft spirit, but after a crisis—perhaps a death, breakup, or financial hardship—your spirit changed to something harder and unyielding? Does your shell look the same, even though you have become bitter or tough on the inside?

Or are you the coffee bean? When things are at their worst, do you get better, make a positive contribution, and change the situation around you?

Norma offered us such honest insight into the fatigue a counselor may face. She finished her contribution by writing, "In a position such as mine, compassion is so important; and when I lose this sense of compassion and when my heart hardens, I sit and remind myself that 'others are feeling this way, too,' and, in

> Like the winds of the sea
> are the ways of fate;
> As we voyage along
> through life,
> 'Tis the set of a soul
> That decides its goal,
> And not the calm or the strife.
>
> Ellen Wheeler Wilcox

this, I do not feel alone and am again able to reconnect with my heart."

I would like to think we might all be like Norma. At times, we may be the egg or the carrot, but at our best, we are coffee beans.

Caution Flags

From my experience in human resources, I have seen the warning signs of "compassion fatigue" in others. A characteristic response is to work harder. With the intention of delivering exceptional care, the individual loses all sense of balance in her life. She works through lunch hours and breaks, foregoes family and social time, and lets spiritual, health, and wellness routines slide. Yet she doesn't necessarily accomplish more. She can't when she is working from a state of exhaustion.

If not avoided, compassion fatigue demands a toll payment, whether in a lack of productivity, absenteeism, short- and long-term disability claims, poor morale, or higher turnover. The need for self-care can become so overwhelming that, sometimes, the worst-case scenario—and only solution, in the mind of the worn-out—is to quit.

The last outcome is a defeat for everyone concerned—even heroes must call out for help occasionally. Look around your community, whatever that community is for you. Be watchful of others' well-being and remind them to slow down or seek out resources available to them at work or in the community. Pay attention to signals asking you to alter direction, reminding you that you may need rescue soon. Here are a few of them:

- Trouble meeting deadlines or decrease in productivity
- Apathy or negativity toward work or people; a decline in motivation
- Prone to more workplace/home accidents or near misses
- Even small changes are upsetting and overreacting to minor situations
- Increase intake of addictive substances
- Difficulty sleeping and/or nightmares; reliving a specific incident

Check in and see how many apply to you. Are you able to alter course and make changes? Are you using all the resources surrounding you to ensure you are taking good care?

From Denial to Admission to Permission

When we left Debra in her role as caregiver for her husband, she was foundering and in denial of her need for self-care. She thought she had to be everything to everyone, especially in a crisis.

> I was the healthy one—I could work, parent, learn to cook, manage the house, and be the strong one that took care of it all. Play healthcare advocate and bitch when necessary—what else could I do? And then I hit a wall, the effects of burnout eating away at my health, perspective, and outlook. I had poured myself into all these other roles and rationalized my lack of self-care as "taking one for the team." Since I could, then I felt I should. I didn't understand at the time that just because we're capable doesn't mean we should. I lived with fear that I hadn't done enough to push the doctors, to get faster appointments, to find the disease and the cure, and put my family back together again.
>
> What I've learned through this incredibly tough life transition is the necessity to live the experience as it shows up and clear away the clutter of busyness and distraction so that you can feel what you really need. Tough transitions bring the opportunity for Growth, Acceptance, and Perspective. Choosing to lean into the opportunity for self-care and compassion is not selfish in the negative sense this word conjures up. It involves being intentional with putting yourself first—and defining what that means for you.
>
> I have learned the most important person to show compassion to is yourself. How can we possibly be authentically compassionate if we don't know what that feels

> like for ourselves? Compassion may mean taking a nap when you feel you really need to get the laundry done. Compassion may be going to the movies and just letting the real world slip away for a couple hours. Compassion may mean sleeping in or saying no. Self-compassion starts with slowing down often enough to feel what you are really feeling and wanting, and knowing that you are enough right now in this moment, and you deserve to be compassionate with yourself. It also means letting go of what no longer serves you, whether that's emotions you've attached to relationships or situations, or self-judgment and blame. Letting go of negative emotions and energy creates space for kindness, patience, and love.
>
> Pay attention to what shows up and seize the opportunities. About a year ago, an opportunity to go to a creative retreat came up and I made the choice to go, and to embrace the opportunity to indulge in what was a complete escape and nurturing experience. It taught me I can go off the grid for four days and my world won't fall apart. It taught me that quiet time, reflective time, time to be grateful and simply open to the learning and experience is self-compassion.

"Live the experience as it shows up and clear away the clutter." We could take these words and apply them to any number of life situations, whatever their gravity. Be present and simplify. Say no. Slow down. Let go.

Debra offers any number of strategies for self-care so that one can regain one's compassionate presence for others, but the essential ingredient is compassion and the recognition that it is needed for oneself.

Kelly, a career counselor, sums it up best by saying, "The world would be a better place if we were able to give ourselves the compassion we can give so freely and unconditionally to others."

To Stifle or Accept

Dr. Jane Dutton is a core researcher at the University of Michigan's Compassion Lab. The lab is made up of researchers and scholars whose mission is to enhance the development and expression of compassion in business.

Dr. Dutton says, "When people know they can bring their pain to work, they no longer have to expend energy trying to ignore or suppress it, and they can more easily and effectively get back to work. Conversely, when you expect people to stifle their emotions, it's very difficult for them to figure out how to focus at work."

I am reminded of Shelley in "Compassionate Belonging." When her brother-in-law was dying, she received "real questions of concern first thing when teachers saw me enter the buildings of a few different schools I work at. There were some teachers who took valuable time from their days to ask and listen and show with their eyes that they truly felt my pain and were thinking about my family and me."

Shelley did not have to put on a false front or create a vacuum between her family life and her work life. Because her life situation and her pain were honored, she was able to be present at both.

What We Cannot Change

My volunteer work in India and Morocco challenged my sensibilities. I helped bathe the disfigured and disenfranchised precious women who would sit on those chilly granite floors in shaking bodies that were so worn and incapacitated they could not entirely aid themselves. I would turn my face so they would not see my tears as I cried for them. I could feel the cold and indifferent floor beneath their delicate, thin skin and fragile bones and I could not change what was. Nor could I compare it to my own standard of living and dying.

When I volunteered at the orphanage in Morocco, I would hold back tears and sometimes even outrage by repeating the mantra we were given on day one from our volunteer coordinator: "It's not your job to compare, criticize, or condemn the standard of care because you are in a different country with different ways. Every day, when you go to your assignment, tell yourself that they are doing the best they can with what they have and you are here to build on what is already done well."

In every situation we encounter, there are conditions beyond our power to change. And so we are left with a choice. How are we to conduct ourselves? Who are we at this moment in time? The answers to these two questions are almost always within our ability to act upon.

The idiom "be in the present moment" sounds poetic—and yet, most people struggle to define what it means in any tangible way. Being "present" occurs when we stop making a comparison of what is here before us to what we have experienced in the past or expect in the future. We are in a neutral and conscious place that allows us to be ready, willing, and of service at this moment in time.

I steadfastly repeated the mantra I had been given. It worked. By the time I left I really had grasped the power of those words at a very personal level.

A Spoonful of Sugar

In "Compassionate Optimism," we discovered that if we have forgotten how to hope or laugh, these can be learned. An article about the Framingham Heart Study published in the *British Medical Journal* suggests that optimism can also be caught.

Between 1983 and 2003, 4,739 people in Framingham, Massachusetts, "were asked how often they experienced certain feelings during the previous week: 'I felt hopeful about the future,' 'I was happy,' 'I enjoyed life,' 'I felt that I was just as good as other people.'"

When the study concluded, the researchers concluded, "... the relationship between people's happiness extends up to three degrees of separation." They found that happiness could be spread like a virus, that "People who are surrounded by many happy people… are more likely to become happy in the future."

Happiness becomes visible the closer we are to someone who is happy. A happy next-door neighbor can raise our happiness by 34 percent. If we have a happy sibling who lives within a mile of us, our happiness will rise by 14 percent. The most significant impact was having a happy friend who lives less than half a mile away. That friend's proximity can shift one's happiness up by 42 percent!

If so, then what is the effect of being in the company of people who are constantly exhibiting tension and stress—or even anger and resentment? In paying close attention to our family, friends, and colleagues and how we interact with one another, we truly can support each other and create a more joyful space between us. Happiness is as catchable as a cold.

A little self-care and happiness go a long way. Here are eight points for enhancing the happiness of yourself and those around you:

1. Find and maintain your sense of humor and optimism
2. Know it's okay to say no—you do not have to be everything to everyone
3. Check in frequently with yourself—do you need support?
4. Practice sustainable compassionate self-care (regarding breaks, time off, hours of work, family, and social activities)
5. Learn routines that promote healthy eating and exercise
6. Reflect on your avocation and where it fits in your life
7. Practice finding your true north through relaxation techniques
8. Find ways to make joy a part of your life

They ask for intention and your commitment to yourself in an ordinary way. Know that you are worthy of help and ask for it, if needed.

If you are experiencing compassion fatigue, then it may seem that some of these suggestions are insurmountable. If so, it may be that you need to seek the support of a professional. These tips are for nurturing the joy of daily living and for cultivating compassionate presence. They ask for intention and your commitment to yourself in an ordinary way.

A Guest House

If we are to hold compassion within our grasp as a way of service for the lonely, sad, disenfranchised, suffering, and afflicted, then it stands to reason that we must care for all of these gone-astray parts of ourselves as well.

Paula Gunn Allen, Native American poet, literary critic, and novelist, advocates that "Healing the self means committing ourselves to a wholehearted willingness to be what and how we are—beings frail and fragile, strong and passionate, neurotic and balanced, diseased and whole, partial and complete, stingy and generous, twisted and straight, storm-tossed and quiescent, bound and free."

Unquestionably, we are a paradox of polarities. But it is being aware of our own pros and cons that allows us to be open to offering compassion to others. Self-compassion requires us to accept that we, too, are fragile and that we live in a world of unrealistic expectations. Perfection is an illusion. We all suffer. At different intervals of our lives, we will suffer various types of pain. We are all a part of the human condition.

Rumi is a renowned and celebrated 13th-century Persian Muslim poet, theologian, and Sufi mystic. His poetry has been read worldwide and has the profound ability to transcend borders and reach into the hearts of readers across all faiths and philosophies.

His poem, "The Guest House," speaks to each of us as we work toward offering ourselves compassion, knowing that we must invite those rough and unattractive spots into our lives to open our hearts and minds.

> This being human is a guest house.
>
> Every morning a new arrival.
>
> A joy, a depression, a meanness, some momentary awareness
>
> comes
>
> as an unexpected visitor.
>
> Welcome and entertain them all!
>
> Even if they're a crowd of sorrows,
>
> who violently sweep your house empty of its furniture,
>
> still treat each guest honorably.
>
> He may be clearing you out for some new delight.
>
> The dark thought, the shame, the malice,
>
> meet them at the door laughing, and invite them in.
>
> Be grateful for whoever comes,
>
> because each has been sent as a guide from beyond.

While speaking at a neonatal care conference last year, a young woman approached me to chat about struggling up against the "guests in her house." This newly graduated nurse informed me that she had come to this conference with her resignation letter written. She was now choosing to tear it up and wanted me to know why.

Obviously passionate about her chosen vocation, she shared her journey through nursing school and then into her recent employment at a hospital. Throughout her education, she had been told she was "too involved with her patients—too soft—too compassionate," and would not be successful because she was not "tough enough."

She had high academic achievements and a warm and loving approach to her patients, yet this once-confident nurse had been led to believe that her character was flawed and that the very essence of who she was wasn't welcomed or appreciated in her work. I know this only too well because, in the early years of my career, I also was told that I would never be successful in human resources if I continued to "wear my heart on my sleeve." It took me a number of years of trial and error to find my personalized foothold and realize that my success only came when I wore that badge of honor on my sleeve without feeling like I had to apologize for it.

I do not believe anyone, given a choice, would choose to stay in any profession that sends the message that self-expression and bringing your whole self to work is not acceptable. After hearing my presentation that afternoon, she had chosen to stand tall, bring all of her compassion—her avocation—proudly to her work, and to stop apologizing for doing so.

Compassionate Presence for Others

It is when we move from a deeply felt compassionate presence for self that we can offer it to another.

"The dying have taught me about living," the elderly gentleman with a most exquisite smile said as I penned his name in my book. I had just concluded speaking at a fundraiser for a local hospice, so the context made his words especially poignant.

"Please, do tell me more," I said. His name was Jack and as I had hoped, he continued his story.

"Well, I think everyone should be a hospice volunteer. I have been one for over 10 years, and I have learned more about living a good life than dying a good death," he said. "It's a privilege to be there, in those final days—or, in many cases, even the final hour—with someone because they are alone, or you are there for their families. You begin to realize how precious the last valuable 30 minutes of life are. When you have been privy to as many end-of-life closing conversations as I have, it changes you with the things people say to a loved one or what the dying say as their last words."

I thought of his words and of how so much can be left unsaid—how visits are cancelled or reconciliations postponed. Jack continued, "I named this 'My 30 Minutes' to remind myself that, if this person—whether it's the store clerk, a co-worker, my friends and family, or even a stranger, basically whomever I am with right now in this moment—was only going to be alive for another 30 minutes, how much differently I would talk or act toward them. This last 30 minutes is not only about the dying; it is now how I live my life and treat the living around me with the same regard and respect."

Jack's words of wisdom are a beacon. His many years of profound listening and witnessing are a testament to the need for not taking another for granted, for not being habituated to each other, and for taking the risk of seeking reconciliation and healing before death ceases that possibility here on earth.

Ellen, a nursing instructor, wrote that she felt "blessed" when she chanced upon witnessing three staff at a residential care facility follow their inner knowing.

> As a resident was nearing the end of her life, Tara, Chad, and Yvonne were at her side—two of them gently

> embracing her while singing her favorite East Coast song, "Mairzy Doats."
>
> A short time earlier, they had noticed her in discomfort and struggling for breath. As they gathered and began to sing to her, she became more at peace. As I left the room, they continued to sing, and within seconds, a smile came over her face, and after one last breath, she passed... there was a beautiful glow in the room, making it impossible to distinguish the angels on high welcoming her from the angels on earth saying their goodbyes.
>
> Later, when I acknowledged the staff for their caring and compassion, they modestly replied, "We were just doing our job." I cherish my presence there that day and it remains one of the highlights of my career.

When we live from compassionate presence, we imbue ourselves with purpose; we offer belonging and hope to others. Presence becomes magical when we let someone know, "you are important and I am here for you" by singing "Mairzy Doats."

What Would Love Do Here?

Writing from a mother's perspective, Marcia says that compassion is in her when she consents to let her heart lead and then she follows, allowing the best part of herself to be present.

> To me, compassion is pure; it is truth and it is without ego, allowing love to be present, and means asking, "What would love do here?" It is to be in love in one's own heart and to share that with the world. I find compassion easier to express in traumatic situations; in family situations—when an adult child, family member, or spouse is angry and upset—compassion requires much more strength. Just yesterday, when my adult daughter was yelling at me that my TV was too loud and that the dryer buzzer was going and that I needed to deal with it, I looked over at her and she was expecting me to defend myself as I had been doing all day; instead, I gazed at her with tenderness and I asked if she was all right. She stopped in mid-stress, her expression changed, and tears filled her eyes. Compassion is seeing the fear, acknowledging the pain, and then witnessing the truth.

Marcia could have taken this conversation in many unproductive directions, yet she paused, took a breath, and realized that this episode had little to do with her. By truly seeing and hearing the other person, she was able to respond and attend to the pain her daughter was experiencing.

What would love do here? This wonderful question packs the equivalent of a heart-based protein bar loaded with additional energy and endurance for our benefit, so that we can move effortlessly into whatever situation we find ourselves and embrace it—sometimes willingly, sometimes reluctantly. This "love" is seeing the person instead of mistaking them for the pain they are suffering.

Leslie's compassionate presence guided a family. Their trauma was not going to have a happy ending and, in order to walk through this tragedy, the family needed someone they could trust.

The story begins when Leslie was a nurse manager in charge over a long weekend. The unit she worked on was a floor for seniors recovering from surgery.

> On Friday, I had a patient, Mr. Roberts, transferred from active care, where he was recovering from a hip replacement. That same night there had been a house fire not far from the university. I heard the news in the morning on the way in to work.
>
> Mr. Robert's wife of fifty years had been severely injured in the blaze. He didn't know this and, by 10 a.m., I had his daughter and son in my office discussing how to handle the situation. Dad was recovering, Mom was on life support, and they didn't know if telling him would compromise his heart and personal recovery.
>
> The daughter didn't want to tell her dad; she wanted to wait until he was stronger. Unfortunately, Mom didn't have this time. I asked to speak with the son. We sat down in my office and I asked him how he was feeling. The fear of losing both parents was evident as, for the past ten years, he had lived far away and had not spent much time with either parent, and his sadness was palpable.
>
> I can still remember my words, "Can you imagine, this man has been married to this woman for 52 years, they have experienced everything together, and this situation, as tragic as it is, isn't our situation—it's theirs. As much as we want to

talk about our needs here, this isn't about us—this is about a man being given the opportunity to say goodbye to the woman he loves and for a woman to have the man she loves at her side when she dies. You and your sister have the power to help that happen or the power to prevent that from happening."

My eyes filled with tears as I said those words. I knew the layers of love and care were hard to pick apart in this situation, but I knew my primary focus was my patient as a whole person. He wasn't a hip replacement. He was a man whose wife was dying and I needed to get him to her, but that decision was not ultimately mine.

Twenty minutes later the ambulance arrived to shuttle Mr. Roberts to see his wife. She died that evening with her husband, daughter, and son at her side. There were many life-changing moments throughout my nursing career, but often the saddest moments were the most whole moments.

Both Marcia and Leslie understood something special. In each situation, emotional and physical pain was paramount, though it was expressed in different ways. And in each situation, Leslie and Marcia understood that it wasn't the pain that was the first priority, it was the person.

From my perspective and experience, when pain and suffering are put ahead of seeing the person, it is easier to disconnect from what is truly happening and important—it is easier to disconnect our humanity and merely function to fix the problem. Leslie's courage in acting with the interest of the real human being first was not a hard decision for her to make. She told me, "Because I accept them as they are—a human, first, who is in need—and secondly, because they are in pain, there is a split second between the two."

This split second carries the traits of an unconscious competent—someone whose intuition and experience are so extensive that decision making becomes second nature for them and they are unconscious of the pause between thinking and doing, between their heart and their mind. When we know what we value; when we know what is most important—as with Leslie, where the human being came first—then this split second is not even distinguishable to the human eye, but only to the human heart, breathing in and out with compassionate presence.

Where We Need to Be

Another contributor worded it as simply accepting people exactly where they are in life, not where they could or should be. Would it not be a peaceful existence if everyone cooperated and were where they could or should be? And yet, who among us is where they could or should be all of the time—if it's possible, I would like to be dropped off on that planet! I know intermittently that I am certainly not and that has caused people in my life angst from time to time.

Robin commented that, in making her contribution, she had been "pushed to analyze" her current situation with her father in-law. In taking the time to be present with herself and seeing through the eyes of compassion, she says, "It feels a lot better now."

> When my in-laws were in their 80s, we looked at options to assist them. My mother-in-law was in the early stages of Alzheimer's and had started to wander away from the family home. We made the decision to have them move in around the corner so we could be accessible and assist in organizing home care as the needs would increase over time. I saw this as an act of kindness. This happened almost two years ago.
>
> As time has passed my father-in-law has become angry and afraid, which has translated into him lashing out at our family when we try to help. He is losing control and doesn't like it, nor can he cope with it. Our family has struggled to find the balance of being kind and putting in boundaries to protect ourselves.
>
> Many times we have wanted to walk away, but we can't. It took a long time but we finally figured out why, and it was because my father-in-law is in pain and no matter how bad it gets we want to help. At first I thought it was guilt bringing us back each time, but it wasn't—it was compassion. Compassion for our fellow man that is afraid. Afraid to die and afraid to live; both are scary for him right now. We continue to give, but do so in a protective way. For instance, we don't visit alone anymore. That way, if he gets mean, the other person can pull us both out of the situation and explain we will come back later.

> At first I thought we were weak because we kept go-ing back for more "abuse" but then, after a long pause, it was not weakness, but compassion that kept bringing us back.

Robin was able to recognize the essence of the man, and to put him at the forefront—to not allow his anger to determine her response, to define him or her. She was then able to move forward with a different viewpoint by humanizing and empathizing with the many deep-rooted fears causing his behavior.

Seeing the person first occurs when we look with compassionate eyes. Sadly, if we do not keep our eyes open, we will miss the opportunity, as it can be such a fleeting moment—one that easily gets entangled in emotions and then can be forever lost. Optimally, the desire to repair the broken becomes a secondary issue—or not an issue at all, in some cases.

Stephanie sums up the essence of presence with such instinct: "Compassion is seeing the other person as they truly are, recognizing them as a fellow brother or sister traveler on the road of life, rather than just another person."

Ask, Then Listen

Compassion can be difficult because we may not be certain of what to do or say when a fellow human being is afflicted with any form of pain. The key is to ask and then listen—and to know that your presence alone will speak volumes for you. This can be done even if your question isn't received with compassion. Like Leslie, you have the opportunity to put aside the fear or the pain at the forefront, and see the human in front of you first. You, therefore, do not need to utter a word—just wait for the answers with respect, appreciation, and love as Bob demonstrated.

Listen completely, listen attentively; listen with your heart so you go beyond the words to feelings and see what is truly important and what this person values most.

In my vocation, I have learned to talk less, take note, and observe, because what is so beautiful about listening is that you can enjoy hearing and experiencing someone's story and point of view. I see every conversation as a new story in a living novel—a new perspective, a new insight and, therefore, rarely will get exhausted from listening.

You are not there to be a trainer or to distribute justice as a judge; you don't have to pretend to be a wise sage or a coach; you just have to connect to the story—that is all. Connect totally and completely to the story.

Another contributor, Debbie, shed light on this measure of pain, saying, "Compassion truly understands how being sick impacts every aspect of a life." By honing our skill in being present, and being still long enough to hear, then the ability to empathically know what comes and what to do next is made easier. By listening intently, we hear the answer.

The Discipline of Listening

Hearing is part of our physiology. Listening, however, is a learned behavior and requires constant self-discipline and practice. If you ever wonder why listening is so difficult for you, then realize you are not alone.

Let math step into the picture here and take a brief bow. We speak, on average, 125 words per minute (wpm). To give you a benchmark, readers for audio books deliver words at 150 to 160 wpm—they speed up a little to keep our attention. But we have the capacity to hear up to 400 wpm. It is because of this cavernous gap between our speaking and hearing that we become distracted so easily and reach a tipping point where we disconnect from the person in front of us. Our minds wander off to do a shopping list, think of the day's agenda, fill in the words of the speaker, or any number of things that distract us from being wholly present.

There are also many biases that may cause us to disengage. A bias, or a preconceived notion, is a form of judgment—and judgment is a tool we use to separate, divide, cleave, and conquer. It requires a self-reflective honesty to confront our capacity for judgment if we have a sincere desire to cultivate presence.

Sometimes there is judgment of the person's appearance or mannerisms; or, we may not find what they are saying of any interest or significance. Perhaps what they say is too close to home or emotionally raw. Yet again, the person may be repeating themselves—something very common with trauma and grief, not to mention aging. Or they may speak slowly and we are so busy filling in their words that we miss what they are actually saying.

We may not agree with what we are hearing. Or we may be distracted by our surroundings. And lastly, I would be remiss if I did not mention the impact of being surrounded by technology 24/7—turn it off and tune in with eye contact to the living person in front of you.

My guidance, if you want to stay present with someone, is fourfold:

- **Listen More than You Speak:** Listening is being peaceful with silence. If you are hearing the sound of your own voice more than 20 percent in a conversation, then you are not being present with the other person—you are being present with yourself. If you must speak, then ask questions to reflect what you have heard so you can deepen the dialogue and carry it further along.

- **Listen for Points:** Points are what the person knows. What vital information is this person giving you concerning times, places, faces, background history, ideas, or expectations? Even if they are not essential, these details will keep your mind engaged and attending to the speaker, instead of wandering.

- **Listen for Values and Beliefs:** Values and beliefs are who the person is. Think of each person as a narrator of his own story and look intently for the plot or theme of the story. Can you identify what his values are? How does he view his environment and those within it? What are his priorities right now? What provides him with a purposeful life? What are his goals and dreams? What does he believe in ethically or spiritually? What keeps him going when he is exhausted and under stress, and, most importantly, what brings him joy and gratitude?

- **Listen for Emotions:** Compassionate listening is hearing what lies beneath the words. Our emotions are ways we express what we cannot always articulate through words. The role of the listener is to affirm these inexpressible feelings. While you listen for the emotions, also watch body language, facial expressions, voice tones, and gestures to give additional clues to verify accurate sentiments.

  To not seek—or, worse, to tune the speaker out—becomes a missed opportunity to reflect to the speaker that you are there, present, and witnessing their story. Reflecting may

> sound like, "You seem very frustrated right now," or, "The joy I am hearing is showing all over you," or, "It's okay to feel confused about this."
>
> One of the best ways to practice is to read emotions when there is no vested interest on your part, such as when you might observe people at a bus stop or an airport, or as a server in a restaurant dealing with a patron.

A bit of visual guidance I offer with respect to being a conscious, compassionate listener comes from a phrase I heard during my trip to India while riding the subway system. Everytime the dual electronic doors would open and close, a recorded female voice would come onto the intercom system and gently remind commuters to "Be Mindful of the Gap" so as not to get caught between train and the platform.

Spinning it around I would remind each of us who want to stay present to "Mind the Gap" between our speaking and thinking speed when listening to another.

The Three-Second Pause

My friend and colleague, Erie Chapman, author of the bestselling books *Radical Loving Care* and *The Caregiver Meditations,* was a CEO at various hospitals throughout his esteemed career. He offers a seemingly simple yet profound resolution to remind us to stay present in the moment with another. Erie generously shares a custom he refers to as a "ritual for the spirit," which he instituted when he was CEO of Baptist Hospital in Nashville. He called upon all caregivers to perform the Three-Second Pause throughout their daily encounters with patients.

> A nurse pauses three seconds before entering one of her patients' rooms, repeats to herself, "This is a person made vulnerable by illness." She then enters the room with grace and an open heart, ready to respond to the needs of a suffering human being. This nurse's pause at the door reflects a lovely if uncommon ritual, taught in some nursing schools and practiced infrequently. Before entering a patient's room, remember the special nature of caregiving. Recall the essential humanity of the person in need. This simple three-second pause could transform the delivery of compassionate care in North America because it reinforces what has been lost in so many organizations: Mindfulness.

The Three-Second Pause can be applied to any encounter, whether at home or the office or coffee shop, whether talking on the phone or writing an email. It is the only tool needed to become a compassionate listener. Who among us cannot find three seconds to stop, pause, and reflect?

To my mind, the pause reflects the twofold nature of compassionate presence because we may use it to be compassionately present for ourselves as well as others. We may use it to listen in to our own well-being, to regain our inner sense of self and so be present when we sit with another.

I turn again to the Sufi mystic Rumi, who offers an insight into finding balance. He wrote, "If [your hand] were always a fist or always stretched open, you would be paralyzed. Your deepest presence is in every small contracting and expanding, the two as beautifully balanced and coordinated as birds' wings."

If we make the error of being open and giving compassion constantly—or closed and not giving compassion—we run the risk of freezing our empathy muscle and commencing a downward spiral to weariness. The Three-Second Pause helps us collect and maintain that beautiful balance Rumi describes.

A Cardboard Box

The ultimate aspiration of the listener is to make certain the person in your presence feels valued, respected, and heard.

Margaret's home burned utterly to the ground. Imagine every picture, gift, book, photo album, and every item you held

> One of the tasks of true friendship is to listen compassionately and creatively to the hidden silences.
>
> John O'Donohue

dear—as well as all the bits and pieces that make up an ordinary home—all gone. The gift, Margaret said, was that everyone, including the family pets, was able to get out without harm.

Because she had lived in her community for many years, boxes of clothing, food, and sundries arrived daily to help Margaret and her family.

The first day she returned to work, her colleagues had care packages to give her. And then she opened one unassuming cardboard box. A cardboard box, bulging at top and bottom, filled with whole wheat pasta in all different shapes and sizes and brands. She broke down in tears.

No, it wasn't that the shock had finally worn off. No, it wasn't that she was among friends and colleagues. No, it wasn't the multitude of care packages and kindness in front of her.

"I am a lover of whole wheat pasta," Margaret tells me, grinning, "and everyone who knows me knows that. I come to work with my lunch and I would go on and on about how much healthier whole wheat pasta is for you and the extra fiber and nutrition, and, of course, it just tastes better! All those years of me talking about it and I never really thought anyone was actually listening to me, but they were. That's what these tears are about. They heard me. They remembered, and they did something about it, and they made me laugh and cry at the same time."

Jack, a nurse, wrote in with his own thoughts about listening: "Compassion to me is taking the time to listen to a patient—no matter how busy I am—holding their hand and letting them know that everything is going to be all right, although it may not be. Compassion goes hand-in-hand with encouragement to get through the difficult times."

I would bet that Jack is using, likely unconsciously, the fourfold method of compassionate listening in order to arrive at this place where he knows to just put everything down and be present in that moment with a fellow human being.

Carol, a director of volunteer services, adds, "Still yourself and absorb another person's issue. Not to own them, or to solve them, or to erase them—just take them in, empathize, listen to the highest degree, and be present with the other person. In true listening, you will know exactly what they need."

Mindful Listening

Dr. Robin Youngson discovered, through listening, exactly what his patient needed. Dr. Youngson lives and works as an anesthetist in New Zealand and is the author of *Time to Care: How to Love Your Patients and Your Job*.

He shares an episode with a patient that was life-changing for him about how he now practices as a doctor in listening for the right words to say. Dr. Youngson was in a consultation with a patient who was going to have to make a difficult decision regarding whether to proceed with surgery.

> Would he take a risk with his life for the sake of receiving a new hip joint and restoring mobility? George had serious coronary artery disease and I was concerned that the stress of surgery and anesthesia might precipitate a fatal heart attack. In my experience, patients had varying attitudes to risk surgery. Some, like George, are philosophical. "I've had a great life but there's no point going on if I can't do the things I want to do. I'm willing to take the risk." Others are risk-averse.
>
> In such a consultation, I try to do my best to serve the patient on their own terms and to allow them to make decisions based on their own values. For a patient, coming to see the specialist in the hospital can be an intimidating experience. Often the greatest worry in the front of the patient's mind is left unspoken. I concluded the appointment with my usual offer, "George, is there anything else I can do for you this afternoon?"
>
> "No thanks, doctor. I appreciate your help." He shook my hand before leaving.
>
> Some months later, I was surprised to learn from the surgeon that George had declined his surgery. I phoned George at home and we had a long conversation. He had declined the surgery because he worried about the burden on his wife of having to nurse him at home after the operation. I asked George why he hadn't raised that concern

> when I saw him in the clinic. "Well, doctor," said George, "it was at the front of my mind but I didn't want to bother you."
>
> Since that time, I have made a subtle alteration to my concluding question. I now ask, "Is there 'something' else I can do for you this afternoon?" Doesn't that feel so different? "Is there 'anything' else?" feels like a dismissive question—a polite "customer service" phrase. In contrast, "Is there something else?" implies that I have an intuitive understanding of a concern still on the patient's mind. Perhaps George might have revealed his concern and the hospital could have arranged a period of rehabilitation or respite care.
>
> How remarkable that life decisions can turn on a single word, even when we try to bring compassion and understanding to our daily work.

Dr. Youngson reached a profound insight by moving from "anything" to "something." He told me in a recent conversation of his mission to "re-humanize" healthcare. He offered that all the right words do not mean anything unless they are offered in a mindful way, unless there is affection and palpable warmth behind them.

We can all take his insight into our daily lives, by mindfully asking the question, "Is there *something* else I can do for you?"

No Detour

Supporting someone with your compassionate presence is mostly being there as the person works through emotions. It's not taking a detour around the person. There are a few tenets that have been useful to me throughout my career in the helping profession. Perhaps a few of them will resonate with you. Each has been written from the perspective of the receiver. I have drawn from the stories presented earlier in the book to share with you how compassionate presence was available for each of the recipients.

Silent Presence

- Reach out to me with a hug, a word, or a handshake to express your love and concern—as Reg did with his one-a-day greeting cards and Edith with her valentines

- Listen without feeling the need to speak, solve anything, or rationalize—as Marcia did when listening to her daughter

- Hold my hand in silence; it can be more comforting than words—as Linda held the hand of the young mother, judgment free

Supportive Presence

- Assist me in making choices that are simple to start with; be a resource for me and a bridge to others when I am ready—as Leslie was for a family dealing with tragedy

- Walk beside me; don't carry me or try to fix me—as I did with Don and found a friend and neighbor

- Lift up my injured spirit; don't take responsibility for what has happened to me or pretend to assume my feelings, and I will find my potential, like Steve did

Sustained Presence

- Don't attempt to rescue me, rather, help me discover my own strength; then I can learn to be independent, play the guitar, and live a full life like Chris does

- Help me explore what I am feeling inside so I don't have to hide my emotions; this way I make peace with my body, mind, and spirit, like Brenda did with her cancer

- Leave the door open by asking me if there is something else you can do for me; I can ask, knowing you see past my pain and see me, and you'll be there no matter what, like Robin did for her father-in-law and Dr. Youngson does with his patients

- Be there for the long haul, because I don't know how long it will take; then I can worry less, take time to heal with my family, and know I am supported, like Jerry was when his child was ill

The Good Samaritan

Action, the natural next step, sounds somewhat easy—once the situation has been taken in, understood, and assessed mentally, emotionally, and perhaps even spiritually. Why, then, don't we take more action in the moment we have been granted? Why do some people act and others do not?

A well-known piece of research conducted at Princeton University looked at this very question in a study named the "Good Samaritan." The name of their study came from the Bible story about two men who walk by and ignore a man who has been beaten, robbed, and is laying half-dead on the side of the road. Shortly thereafter, a third man, known as a Samaritan in biblical times, stops and helps the injured man.

The Princeton study focused on what might make one person stop, yet not another. Seminary students were the unwitting subjects of the study. They were all instructed that they would be giving a practice sermon in another building. Half of the students were assigned The Good Samaritan story as the topic of their sermon. The other half—the control group—were given a different topic. The students were given a bit of time to prepare for their practice sermon and then were asked to proceed to the evaluation building to deliver their sermon.

While walking to the building, each student encountered a man who was half-conscious, bedraggled, and slumped over in a lane, moaning in pain, and who would cough twice to draw their attention. The researchers had varied the level of urgency for each test subject. Some had been told they were late and needed to rush. Others had been told they had only enough time to get there. The rest had been told they had time to spare but should leave now. Once the subjects arrived at the building, they proceeded to give their sermon and then were asked to fill out a questionnaire.

The results were startling. Overall, 40 percent of the students had offered some level of assistance to the gentleman in distress, but the fact that a student was to give a sermon on The Good Samaritan did not seem to determine his decision to help. Time, or the perceived lack of time, seemed to be the determining factor. Where students had been told they had plenty of time, 63 percent of students in that group helped the "victim;" where students had been told that time was of a medium urgency, 45 percent of the group helped; but where students had been told they were running late, only 10 percent of the group stopped to help.

The Time We Save

The moral of the story is ironic. Even students with the best of intentions—enrolled in a faith-based class, and en route to deliver a sermon about helping those in need—did not stop when they believed they did not have enough time.

This study showcases just how difficult it can be to maneuver around our enslavement to the clock and how it affects our very presence with another human being. Time may be one of our worst enemies when it comes to committing kind and compassionate acts.

Sadly, in the researchers' summary, it said, "… ethics become a luxury as the speed of our daily lives increases." Today, everyone is dealing with time constraints. And yes, it can take seconds and minutes of our time to be present. It can make us detour from our hurried route. But, when we make the choice to be present, it can make all the difference in the world.

And yet it also seems that, if we are mindful when we do something—if we take that extra three-second pause, as Erie Chapman recommends, or even a three-minute pause—we may save ourselves ten minutes, or thirty, or even an hour somewhere else. The need to circle back to an issue with another person may become less urgent or even unnecessary when they feel valued and heard the first time. Impatience can be the death of compassion.

The Time We Have

Ellen is a nurse educator who teaches her students to do backrubs, offer a night snack, or deliver hot facecloths for hands and face as a bedtime routine for patients. She testifies that she learned early on that putting in a few extra minutes up front to settle patients saved her rings on the call button, resulted in fewer requests for sleep medications, and created more peaceful shifts. When her colleagues tell her they don't have time to do backrubs, she tells them, "You don't have time not to."

In this precious time we have together, presence brings resonance to our encounters—a deep chime that reverberates like the tone of a bell. It is our inherent capacity to listen and pay close attention to intuitive promptings, so that we may be guided in what to say or do next.

Compassionate presence is accepting and offering in the moment the three treasures that Bob revealed we seek: respect, appreciation, and love.

If you give a daffodil sunshine, it gently opens up; if you listen to someone, the same thing happens. Perhaps, quite simply, compassionate presence brings happiness.

"What day is it?" asked Pooh.

"It's today," squeaked Piglet.

"My favorite day," said Winnie the Pooh.

Chapter 8

A Movement Forward

*There are risks and costs to action.
But they are far less than the long range risks
of comfortable inaction.*

John F. Kennedy

What is Your Sari?

Mother Teresa once met a woman wrapped in an exquisite sari. It cost 800 rupees; the saris the Sisters wear cost 8.

The woman wished to help, and, after much conversation, Mother Teresa respectfully suggested that the next time the woman purchased a sari, she could buy one whose worth was 500 rupees. With the remaining 300, she might purchase saris for the poor. The woman gladly did so. And, as time went by, she found that the less she paid for her saris, the more she had to share.

Who among us has not found an item lost its glamour once purchased? Who among us hasn't smiled when we've seen the pleasure a baby gets from splashing water or when we remember a lovely walk in a verdant forest?

The woman was never asked to continue decreasing the amount she paid. She did so on her own and eventually ended up buying saris for 100 rupees. It was a choice she made because she found it changed her life for the good. In letting go of what we perceive we value most, we find our truer self—our more compassionate self.

Compassion in action is not all or nothing. We do not need to render ourselves naked, impoverished, saddened, or struggling. Compassion can be offered in ways that make you feel comfortable, one sari at a time.

There is a deli in my hometown that sells sandwich tokens for patrons to give out to the homeless. When you buy a lunch, buy a token. Or pack your lunch today and buy a token. In Oregon, a dry cleaner posts a sign that, if you need clothes cleaned for a job interview and are disadvantaged, they will clean them for free. The ways to offer compassion are as myriad as your imagination, your means, and your energy. For some, a "sari" might be smoking fewer cigarettes or buying one less latte or glass of wine and distributing the difference. It might be pausing for three seconds before you speak.

I would also invite you to have a genuine conversation with the homeless gentleman or lady for whom you bought the token. Or spend a day at a food bank. You will soon discover it means one thing to donate cans of food for the warehouse and yet another to personally hand out a bag of groceries to a family of four.

It is when we give of ourselves that we are actually giving.

Compassion into Action

I began this book with my Koan: *What is compassion?*

It was a question that absorbed and consumed my thoughts. I have now found my peace and a sense of both lightness and strength from my search. For me, compassion feels like an alive and awake presence. It is something that breathes life into everything. I believe that when we practice compassion as a devotion, we gather in optimism, belonging, and purpose. We dwell in compassionate presence. I think I have come to this understanding through listening to, and hearing, thousands of voices, each an individual expression of compassion.

There may be much truth to the saying that the longest journey we will ever take in our lifetime is the one from our head to our heart. There is what we think and what we feel. The question is, will we take action?

The unfailing answer to that question is another: *What would compassion do here?* By asking that question and listening for the answer, we are led to understand how we need to show up; in other words, how we might think, speak, and act differently.

There has been a growing movement to bring kindness and compassion to the forefront of public and private discussion, to recognize that these qualities are vital—not just so we survive, but so we may thrive in our work, our homes, and our world.

Compassion and Balloons

I remember that crisp winter afternoon in New Delhi and the childish delight I shared with the women residents. Endeavoring to set down what I have learned has been an exercise in floating colorful balloons in the air and seeing which ones I catch or playfully toss to someone else, which ones float through the sky to places unknown, and which ones fall to the ground, where I may gently pick them up. While I wrote this book, I had a touchstone on my desk as a friendly cue. This warm orange-and-brown-hued agate stone fits in the palm of my hand, and has etched across its center, "Compassion is the art of caring."

I hope that you, too, may be inspired with questions and seek answers. I wish you may be both playful and peaceful in your journey and that you may be inspired to turn your own beautiful expression of compassion into action, into something that is uniquely and vibrantly you, into something that you can share with the world.

Oneness comes naturally when a common aim is shared, even if it is as simple and humble as keeping balloons aloft in the air.

Contemplative Guide

Action will remove the doubts that theory cannot solve.

Tehyi Hsieh

What we plant in the soil of contemplation,
we shall reap in the harvest of action.

Meister Eckhart

A Movement Toward Taking Responsibility

It is now your turn to float a few of your own colorful balloons in the air to see which ones float to the sky and which fall to the ground. Compassion is not a commodity; you can't trade it on the stock market, it does not come with an expiration date, nor is it of limited supply. You can't lose it when you use it. It multiplies upon use which showcases its infinite and significant value.

We cannot shift our current state of affairs personally and globally unless there is a conscious effort to move from self-indulgence to self-efficacy. The goal of this contemplative guide is to help you reflect upon your own learning and make choices to take action.

It is designed to ask you thought-provoking questions to

contemplate in each chapter. As well, each chapter offers multiple actionable steps for consideration. Taking steps to join the compassionate movement starts within you. Once you have determined what compassion looks like for you, the next step is the focused question, *What would compassion do here?*

It is highly suggested to use your book as a reference. Begin a journal to write down reflections, questions, and inspirations throughout each of the chapters. The Contemplative Guide can be explored individually or in a group setting.

Chapter One
A Commitment

Questions to Contemplate

1. What is your definition of compassion? Is compassion like a virus—can it be caught and spread around?

2. Describe the bright flame inside of you.

3. Mother Placid offered a profound possibility when she said, "Compassion is witnessed in the middle." Can compassion offer a way for us to change the isolating space between us, to thrive, not just survive?

4. How has compassion been an *alive* presence in your life, your work, or your team?

Putting Compassion into Action
— A Movement Forward

Make a Commitment: When we breathe our last breath, we each want to know we have lived a good life; a life that matters, of knowing that we are all in this together as a global community. Reflect on what gives you—or is required to inspire you—to make a further commitment to hold compassion as a way of living in the world.

Create a Koan: If you could narrow all of your questions down to one—to your Koan—in order to "weaken the persistent logical mind," what would your Koan be?

Begin a Dialogue: Invite others in your life and work to hold a dialogue on what compassion means to them. Start a meet-up group to further explore the intricacies of compassion's influence in all aspects of one's life and work. Create a safe environment in which to listen and hold authentic conversations.

Chapter Two
A Devotion

Questions to Contemplate

1. At some point we all ask "why is this happening?" When have you asked "Why?" How did you find a peaceful answer?

2. What are you devoted to in your life and in your work?

3. If you think of compassion as a verb, what words do you connect to it?

4. If you applied your version of the Golden Rule to your life and work, would you have handled a particular situation differently? How would you live your daily life differently if you applied the compass of compassionate reciprocity to your actions and decisions?

Putting Compassion into Action
— A Movement Forward

Discern Your Own Devotion: How do you worship? What form does your contemplative practice take? Set an intention to explore compassion as a potential "devotion" in your life.

- Read through each version of The Golden Rule. Put aside the relationship to any particular affiliation and only concentrate on the message itself. From the 13 versions of The Golden Rule, journal particular words or phrases that resonate with you more than others.

- Learn more about someone else's beliefs or denomination by reading or attending a service.

- Notice the diversity in your workplace and in your social circles. Review ways to be more inclusive of different faiths and traditions.

Explore the Charter: Check out www.charterforcompassion.org or www.childrenscharterforcompassion.com and review the charters. Deepen your understanding of the charter language. Consciously devote yourself to, and record, 21 days of living The Golden Rule every day in every way.

Practice Non-Judgment: Choose four people in your personal life or at work who require your compassion. Practice the Just Like Me meditation. What did you notice when you did this exercise?

Chapter Three
A Science

Questions to Contemplate

1. Can compassion be qualified and quantified? Is it important?
2. Is your country on the World Giving Index? If you were interviewed for this Index about your charitable actions in the past 30 days by way of financial donations, volunteering, and helping strangers, how would you answer them personally and professionally?
3. When you do a compassionate act, do you experience "helper's high?" What does it feel like?
4. How important is touch to you? How does it support compassion?

Putting Compassion into Action
– A Movement Forward

Feel Compassion: Journal your thoughts on the Thomas Aquinas quote: "I would rather feel compassion than know the meaning of it." Next time you commit an act of compassion, note what you feel emotionally and physically. How long did it last?

Practice 15 Minutes a Day: Dr. Mongrain's comments that, "Empathy needs to be practiced" and that doing acts of kindness for as little as 15 minutes a day can change your viewpoint. Take up the challenge in your life and work to do one kindness per day for one week.   Record in your journal any long-term affects after the week.

Jumpstart Yourself: Oxytocin is there, waiting to be released; it's like a spark plug for igniting you with inspiration. Revisit the three ways to jumpstart your compassionate self (affection, contemplative practices, and recalling happy memories). Write down one attainable goal on each step you would like to add into your life and work.

Chapter Four
Compassionate Optimism

Questions to Contemplate

1. Do you consider yourself an optimist or pessimist? Explore what factors in your life may have influenced one or the other.

2. Optimism is taking responsibility for the energy and vitality you bring to the space surrounding you. What kind of optimistic force do you bring to your space, whether at home, work, a coffee shop, or the mall?

3. Name the 10 percent curve balls that life has thrown you. What gifts have they brought into your life? What will you do with your 40 percent choice to be optimistic?

4. To fully value the power of compassionate optimism, it is helpful to know people who embody its qualities. Who are people in your life and work who demonstrate optimism?

Putting Compassion into Action
– A Movement Forward

Climb more Mountains: Revisit the story of Amon and the Egyptian village. How much awareness do you have of your ghosts and personal and professional "ogres?" What are your "What Might Have Been's" in your life and work? Make a plan of how you will climb up the mountain and face them. List what support, from who, and when, you will need to accomplish this climb and how you will know when you got to the top.

Increase Positive Interactions: Challenge yourself to be a silent observer of those around you. Notice the amount of positive and negative interactions in your home, workplace, or community. For one week only observe negatives. The following week only observe positives. What did you notice mentally, emotionally, physically, and even spiritually in each week? Journal your thoughts. Commit to increase your positive interactions with others daily.

Count Your Blessings: Begin a Gratitude Journal and record the areas of your life and work that you are grateful for each day for 21 days. What will you do differently in your life to bring more gratitude and joy into it?

Chapter Five
Compassionate Purpose

Questions to Contemplate

1. A job description is like a jacket you put on when you walk in the door of your work. Does your jacket fit like a straitjacket—restricting, confining? Do you wear this jacket as though someone had made it entirely for you? Does putting it on change your personality into someone you don't really intend or like to be?

2. Your "is" is what makes people want to be in your presence. Do people have a little more joy because you came along today, or do they have a little less? Do you come to your life's work meanspirited, show open disdain for your tasks, and treat others with disrespect, or the contrary? Do you show up and contribute emotionally, intellectually, and optimistically?

3. In the "Tale of Two Pots," was there a personal message that stood out for you?

4. Describe your vocation and your avocation. Is one missing in your life? Do you apply both and bring your whole self to your tasks whether at home or at work?

Putting Compassion into Action
— A Movement Forward

Find Your "Is": Take the time to unwrap your "is." Purpose comes wrapped up in one's approach to what one does, how one shows up, and how one "is." Describe your "is" in detail and what you would like to do to expand it further.

Weave Purpose into Life and Work: Purpose is the sustainable energy found, often hidden, in one's livelihood or daily life responsibilities. Create your life description by jotting down some key areas you are responsible for in your family and personal life. If you have a job description from work, take it home and look at it more deeply and with different eyes. As you review your responsibilities, ask yourself, "How could I bring more compassionate purpose to this particular responsibility I have?" Rewrite your description and put it into action immediately.

Start with a Beginner's Mind: To learn something new, you have to let go of what no longer serves you to make room for new concepts. There is no pressure to change your mind; only to have an open mind—a beginner's mind. Pick something in your life or work that you would like to practice a beginner's mind on. Learn more about this subject, read, research, ask questions, attend an event, or find a mentor. Journal if you were able to let go of something so you could replace it with something new.

Chapter Six
Compassionate Belonging

Questions to Contemplate

1. What do "belonging" and "compassionate belonging" mean to you? How do they differ in your life and work?

2. "I am because of who we are" is the South African philosophy of Ubuntu. When have you witnessed Ubuntu in your community? What does Ubuntu mean to you in regards to creating a sense of belonging? Can this be applied to your work?

3. Are you a compassionate consumer? Buying items that are

created by child labor, that are not fairly traded, or have a detrimental environmental impact would be contrary to the value of compassion. Do your values align with the products you purchase?

4. Abraham Lincoln was known as a kind and compassionate man who, when confronted with an individual he did not initially care for, would say, "I must get to know him better." Who do you need to get to know better?

Putting Compassion into Action
– A Movement Forward

Become a Compassionate Citizen: As a citizen you have a sense of the wellness of your community. If you took action, how could you further build trust, foster interconnectedness, and cultivate inclusion to create cities where compassion is the sustainable energy lighting your neighborhood?

Ask *What Would Compassion Do?:* When you attend work and social events or walk down the street, you bump into opportunities to create a sense of belonging for yourselves and others. Ask yourself, "What would compassion do?" over the next four weeks and record in your journal positive actions you took to bring this phrase to life.

Become Someone People Can Turn To: Loneliness and isolation are factors everyone experiences at some point in life. Is there someone in your community you can reach out to and close the gap with your presence to create connection and belonging? Review each of the thoughts on how to bridge the gap (create a new circle of friendship, reach beyond your current boundaries, ensure everyone feels valued, respected, and heard). Select one item from each section you would like to practice in both your life and your work. Journal your experience.

Chapter Seven
Compassionate Presence

Questions to Contemplate

1. Compassionate presence is twofold. It is holding firmly to an unhindered commitment of being present to oneself. It is holding a sacred space for another: *You are important and I am here for you.* Contemplate each of these in your own life. What has been the impact of presence, or a lack of presence, in your life and work?

2. How aware are you of yourself at this very moment? What gets in your way of being in the present moment?

3. In the story of the Coffee Bean, which one are you: a carrot, an egg, or a coffee bean? Are you one at work and another in your personal life?

4. If you applied the principle of "My 30 Minutes" to conversations you have with family, friends, colleagues, and strangers, how will you act differently?

Putting Compassion into Action
– A Movement Forward

Be Compassionate to Yourself: Self-compassion requires you to accept that perfection is an illusion. Check in with yourself by reviewing the six caution flags. Alter your course immediately if necessary. Revisit the eight points for enhancing happiness. Pick one to begin now. Record your successes in your journal.

Mindfully Listen: Listening is a learned behavior and requires constant self-discipline. Begin to pay closer attention between your listening and thinking speed. Over four weeks, practice one of the fourfold listening techniques to stay present (Listen More than You Speak, Listen for Points, Listen for Values and Beliefs, Listen for Emotions). Record in your journal your successes and observations for each week.

Avoid Detours: Supporting someone with your compassionate presence is being there as the person works through emotions. Practice each of the three presence tenets (Silent, Supportive, and Sustained) when an opportunity arises in your personal or work environment. What did you notice changed in your interaction with the receiver as you applied a tenet? Journal your experience of what worked, what challenges you had, and how you would adjust your approach next time.

Sources

Chapter 1/ A Commitment
Selected Bibliography

González-Balado, José Luis. *Stories of Mother Teresa*. Liguori Publications, 1983.

Mother Teresa. *No Greater Love*. Navator, CA: New World Library, 1989.

Mother Teresa. *Mother Teresa, Her Essential Wisdom*. New York: Fall River Press, 2006.

Spink, Kathryn. *For the Brotherhood of Man Under the Fatherhood of God, Her Missionaries of Charity and Her Co-Workers*. Don Mills: Collins Publishers, 1981.

Vazhakala, Fr. Sebastian, M.C. *Life With Mother Teresa: My Thirty-Year Friendship with the Mother of the Poor*. Servant Publications, 2004

Doig, Desmond. *Mother Teresa: Her People and Her Work*. Harper & Row, Publishers 1976.

Serrou, Robert. *Teresa of Calcutta*. McGraw-Hill Book Company, 1980.

Schaaf, Kathe, Kay Lindahl, Kathleen S. Hurty, PhD, and Reverend Guo Cheen. *Women, Spirituality and Transformative Leadership, Where Grace Meets Power*. Woodstock, VT: Sky-Light Paths Publishing, 2012.

Salzberg, Sharon. *Loving Kindness: The Revolutionary Art of Happiness*. Boston & London: Shambhala Library, 2004.

Web Resources

The official site of the Mother Teresa of Calcutta Center: www.motherteresa.org

Cross-Cultural Solutions offers opportunities in the field of international volunteer travel: www.crossculturalsolutions.org

Chapter 2/ A Devotion
Selected Bibliography

Underhill, Evelyn. Mysticism, *The Preeminent Study in the Nature and Development of Spiritual Consciousness*. New York: Double Day, 1990.

Pilgrim, Peace. Peace Pilgrim: Her Life and Work in Her Own Words. Santa Fe, New Mexico: Ocean Tree Books, 2003.

Nouwen, Henri J.M., *The Way of the Heart*. First Ballentine Books, 1981.

Rushnell, Squire. *When God Winks at You, How God Speaks Directly to You Through the Power of Coincidence*. Nashville: Thomas Nelson Inc, 2006.

The Meaning of the Holy Q'uran. Beirut: Al-Aalami Publications, 2007.

Armstrong, Karen. *12 Steps to a Compassionate Life*. New York: Anchor Books, 2011.

Armstrong, Karen. *A Case for God*. New York: Knopf, 2009.

Tolle, Eckhart. *The Power of Now: A Guide to Spiritual Enlightenment*. Vancouver: Namaste Publishing, 1997.

HH Dalai Lama and Howard C. Cutler. *The Art of Happiness: A Handbook for Living*. New York: Penquin Putnam, 1998.

Sanguin, Bruce. *Darwin, Divinity, and the Dance of the Cosmos: An Ecological Christianity*. Kelowna: Wood Lake Publishing, 2007.

Marshall, Joseph M. *The Lakota Way*. New York: Penquin, 2002.

Khechog, Nawang. *Awakening Kindness: Finding Joy Through Compassion for Others*. New York: Astria Books, 2010.

Bachelor, Stephen. *Buddhism Without Beliefs: A Contemporary Guide to Awakening*. New York: The Berkley Publishing Group, 1997.

Bhaktivedanta, A. C. *Bhagavad-Gita As It Is*. U.K: Bhaktivedanta Book Trust, 1984.

Web Resources

The Golden Rule poster is now on permanent display at the United Nations in New York. To view or order the poster:
www.scarboromissions.ca/Golden_rule/poster_order.php

To sign the Charter for Compassion and to learn about activities and events inspired by its ideals: www.charterforcompassion.org

For more on the Children's Charter for Compassion and how your school can sign up: www.childrenscharterforcompassion.com

Inspired by the work of Mahatma Gandhi and Dr. Martin Luther King, Jr., A Season for Nonviolence is a national 64-day campaign in honor of their vision for an empowered, peaceful world. www.64days.org

Chapter 3/ A Science
Selected Bibliography

Zak, Paul J., Dr. *The Moral Molecule: The Source of Love and Prosperity.* New York: Dutton, 2012.

Luks, Allan, and Peggy Payne. *The Healing Power of Doing Good: The Health and Spiritual Benefits of Helping Others.* Lincoln NE: iUniverse Inc, 2001.

Gottman, John M, PhD, and Nan Silver. *The Seven Principles for Making a Marriage Work.* New York: Three Rivers Press, 1999.

Mannion, James. *Essentials of Philosophy: The Basic Concepts of the World's Greatest Thinkers.* New York: Fall River Press, 2006.

Keltner, Dacher. *Born to be Good: The Science of a Meaningful Life.* New York: WW Norton & Company, 2009.

Gladwell, Malcolm. *The Tipping Point: How Little Things Can Make a Big Difference.* New York: Back Bay Books, 2000.

Post, G. Stephen. *The Hidden Gifts of Helping: How the Power of Giving, Compassion, and Hope Can Get Us Through Hard Times.* San Francisco: Jossey-Bass, 2011.

Web Resources

The World Giving Index is only one of many charts at this website: http://chartsbin.com/view/vfp

The American Enterprise is a leading conservative think-tank. Arthur C. Brooks' article is found here: http://www.american.com/archive/2008/march-april-magazine-contents/a-nation-of-givers

The Center for Compassion and Altruism Research (CCARE) at Stanford University has created a compassion wiki: http://ccare.stanford.edu/research/compassion-wiki/

as well as a compassion database: http://ccare.stanford.edu/research/compassion-database/

For articles relating to research on the brain and altruism:
http://greatergood.berkeley.edu/article/item/the_compassionate_instinct
http://www.sciencedaily.com/releases/2002/07/020718075131.htm

The Greater Good Science Center "studies the psychology, sociology, and neuroscience of well-being, and teaches skills that foster a thriving, resilient, and compassionate society." www.greatergood.berkeley.edu

The Compassion Lab is a center for positive organizational scholarship which "creates research, resources, insights, and inspiration related to compassion at work." www.thecompassionlab.com

For more on **Dr. Marcial Losada,** leading researcher on the positive to negative ratio: www.losadalineconsulting.net

The Fraser Institute, a leading conservative think-tank and research organization, released its findings on generosity: http://www.fraserinstitute.org/uploadedFiles/fraser-ca/Content/research-news/research/publications/generosity-index-2012.pdf

New York's Stony Brook University Center for Medical Humanities, Compassionate Care, and Bioethics: www.stonybrook.edu/bioethics/ and its 2012 biennial report: http://www.stonybrook.edu/bioethics/biennialreport.pdf

The Dalai Lama Center for Peace and Education in Vancouver, Canada: www.dalailamacenter.org

For more information on the heart/mind connection and building resilience: www.heartmath.org

Friendship between Bella (a dog) and Tara (an elephant) http://channel.nationalgeographic.com/wild/unlikely-animal-friends/videos/the-elephant-and-the-dog/

Snaggle Puss (a cat) adopts Bubbles (a baby rabbit) http://www.care2.com/greenliving/cat-adopts-rabbit-video.html

Moko the dolphin assists two pygmy whales http://news.bbc.co.uk/2/hi/7291501.stm

Elephants and mourning http://www.dailymail.co.uk/news/article-2270977/Elephants-really-grieve-like-They-shed-tears-try-bury-dead--leading-wildlife-film-maker-reveals-animals-like-us.html

Chapter 4/ Compassionate Optimism
Selected Bibliography

Dickens, Charles. *A Tale of Two Cities*. Penquin Classics, 2003.

Seligman, Martin, Dr. *Learned Optimism: How to Change Your Life and Your Mind*. New York: Pocket Books, 1991.

Beattie, Melody. *CoDependent No More: How to Stop Controlling Others and Start Caring For Yourself*. Hazelden, 1986.

Clapham, Ward. *Lead Big: Discovering the Upside of Unconventional Leadership*. Vancouver: Fairwinds Press, 2011.

Csikszentmihalyi, Mihaly. *Flow: The Psychology of Optimal Experience*. New York: HarperCollins, 1990.

Doidge, Norman. *The Brain That Changes Itself: Stories of Personal Triumph from the Frontiers of Brain Science*. New York: Penquin Books, 2007.

Lyubomirsky, Sonja Dr. *The How of Happiness: A New Approach to Getting the Life You Want*. New York: Penquin Books, 2007.

Bateman, Kody. *Promptings: Your Inner Guide to Making a Difference*. Salt Lake City: Eagle One Publishing, 2010.

Emmons, Robert. E. *Thanks!: How Practicing Gratitude Can Make You Happier*. New York: Houghton Mifflin, 2008.

McIvor, Olivia. *Four Generations, One Workplace: Sharing in the Information Age,* Vancouver: Fairwinds Press, 2011.

Fredrickson, Barbara L. *Positivity: Top-Notch Research Reveals the 3-1 Ratio That Will Change Your Life*. New York: MJF Books, 2009.

Web Resources

www.happiness.org is a Facebook page devoted to sharing and spreading happiness.

A website devoted to sharing inspiration and uplifting news: http://www.dailygood.org/index.php?pg=about

Learn more about the Positive Tickets program at www.positivetickets.com

For more on Positive Psychology: www.positivepsychologynews.com

A website devoted to sharing inspiration and uplifting news: http://www.dailygood.org/index.php?pg=about

To catch the happiness bug: www.goodvirus.org

For more on gratitude and heart-inspired living: www.gratitudepower.net

www.Onbeing.org is a radio show that asks: "**What does it mean to be human?**" and explores answers "in all the variety, richness, and complexity with which they find expression in contemporary lives."

A non-profit organization dedicated to the practice of kindness in everyday life: www.spreadkindness.org

Chapter 5/ Compassionate Purpose
Selected Bibliography

Lewis Ralph, and John Nobel. *Servant-Leadership: Bringing the Spirit of Work to Work*. United Kingdom: Forge House, 2008.

Dyer, Wayne W. *Inspiration: Your Ultimate Calling*. Carlsbad, Ca: Hay House, 2006.

Lee, Fred. *If Disney Ran Your Hospital: 9 ½ Things You Would Do*

Differently. Health Forum, 2007.

Barks, Coleman. *A Year With Rumi: Daily Readings*. HarperOne, 2006.

De Saint-Exupéry, Antoine, *The Little Prince*. Hertfordshire: Wordsworth Editions, 1995.

Behar, Howard. *It's Not About the Coffee: Leadership Principles from a Life at Starbucks*. New York: Penquin Books, 2007.

McIvor, Olivia. *The Business of Kindness: Creating Work Environments Where People Thrive*. Vancouver: FairWinds Press, 2006.

Frost, Robert. *Two Tramps in Mud Time: A New Poem*. Spiral Press, 1934.

Web Resources

Free the Children is a website and charitable organization full of inspiration and ideas for empowering and involving youth:

www.freethechildren.com

http://www.freethechildren.com/domestic-programming/our-model-we-day/

http://www.freethechildren.com/we-school/

Hearts in Healthcare is an inspirational community of health professionals, students, patient advocates, health leaders, and many others who are champions for compassionate care. www.heartsinhealthcare.com

Erie Chapman (the Three-Second Pause) offers compassionate and inspiring reflections: "Radical Loving Care – The Journal of Sacred Work": http://journalofsacredwork.typepad.com/journal_of_sacred_work/

Kind Media Foundation is a non-profit organization dedicated to "supporting and empowering meaningful social projects." www.kindmedia.com

People for Good is a coalition to get Canadians to be nicer by donating good deeds to each other: www.peopleforgood.ca

The goal is to perform one million acts of kindness in your lifetime. By starting with kind thoughts and encouragement within your circle of influence, you just might reach it: www.onemillionactsofkindness.com

"The Foundation for a Better Life creates public service campaigns to communicate the values that make a difference in our communities. These uplifting messages, utilizing television, movie theaters, billboards, radio and the internet, model the benefits of a life lived by positive values."
www.values.com

Chapter 6/ Compassionate Belonging
Selected Bibliography

Powell, John. *Why Am I Afraid To Tell You Who I Am?* Texas: Argus Communications, 1969.

Goleman, Daniel. *Social Intelligence: The Revolutionary New Science of Human Relationships.* New York: Bantam Dell, 2006.

Ferrucci, Peiro. *The Power of Kindness: The Unexpected Benefits of Leading a Compassionate Life.* New York: Penquin Group, 2006.

Merton, Thomas. *The Pocket Thomas Merton.* Boston & London: New Seeds, 2005.

Carroll, Michael. *Awake at Work.* Boston: Shambhala Publishing, 2004.

Umrigar, Thrity. *The Space Between Us: A Novel.* New York: Harper Collins, 2005.

Buscaglia, Leo. *Loving Each Other: The Challenge of Human Relations.* New York: Random House, 1984.

Dojc, Yuri, and Sharon Henderson. *Honour: Their Stories, Our History.* Mississauga: Chartwell Master Care, 2010.

Wheatley, Margaret J. *Turning to One Another: Simple Conversations to Restore Hope to the Future.* Berkley, Ca: Berrett-Koehler, 2002.

Mandela, Nelson. *Long Walk to Freedom.* New York: Holt, *Rinehart and*

Winston, 2000.

Kielburger, Craig and Marc Kielburger. *Me to We: Finding Meaning in a Material World.* New York: Fireside, 2006.

HH Dalai Lama and Howard Cutler. *The Art of Happiness at Work: The Conversation Continues About Job, Career, and Calling.* New York: River Head Books, 2003.

Sher, Barbara. *Live the Life You Love In Ten Easy Step-by-Step Lessons,* New York: Dell Publishing, 1996.

Web Resources

Ben's bells are now being hung every day of the year. To read this emotional, inspiring story: www.bensbells.org

The Compassion Games are designed to make communities better places to live. www.compassiongames.org

The Global Coherence Initiative is a project launched by the Institute of Heart Math to "unite people in heart-focused care and intention, to facilitate the shift in global consciousness from instability and discord to balance, cooperation and enduring peace." www.glcoherence.org

In April 2008, Seattle hosted The Seeds of Compassion. It was "an historic series of public gatherings, discussions, and workshops that galvanized individuals, networks, and organizations around the world." http://www.seedsofcompassion.org/default.asp

Canadians for Compassion are on a mission inspired by the Charter for Compassion and its evocation of The Golden Rule: www.canadians4compassion.org

Carry Kindness Forward is an "intentional blog" that shares stories and tips to make kindness even more present in our everyday lives:

www.carrykindnessforward.com

Kiva offers an affordable way to do kindness and create an opportunity for someone else: www.kiva.org

The World Kindness Movement hopes to foster goodwill and understanding among all peoples. www.theworldkindnessmovement.org

The Kindness Foundation mission is "everyone deserves kindness; it is essential for us to thrive. Try Some!" www.kindnessfoundation.com

Visit Louisville or Seattle and explore their compassionate initiatives:
http://www.louisvilleky.gov/CompassionateCity/
www.compassionateseattle.org

Read about The Compassionate Cities movement at the Charter for Compassion website: http://charterforcompassion.org/news-and-events/article/130

Compassionate Action Network is "a worldwide network founded upon and inspired by the Charter for Compassion." Its mission is to build "a global movement that brings the Charter for Compassion to life."
http://compassionateaction.org/global-compassion-movement

The Greater Vancouver Compassion Network (GVCN) is "a non-profit network of institutions, organizations, working groups and individuals committed to furthering compassionate engagement and conduct in our communities." www.gvcn.ca

Hand in Hand is "a non-denominational and politically independent charity organization" assisting "the poorest of the poor in the underdeveloped regions of India." www.handinhand.at

"Through our small collective acts, "we hope to transform ourselves and the world." www.servicespace.org

"The International Working Group on Compassionate Organizations is made up of people dedicated to fostering cultures of compassion". www.compassionorg.net.

Compassionate Mind is a Foundation that aims to promote wellbeing through the scientific understanding and application of compassion. www.compassionatemind.co.uk

Chapter 7/ Compassionate Presence
Selected Bibliography

Picoult, Jodi. *Second Glance*. New York: Washington Square Press, 2004.

Youngson, Robin, Dr. *Time to Care: How to Love Your Patients and Your Job*. New Zealand: Rebelheart Publishers, 2012.

Chapman, Erie. *Radical Loving Care: Building the Healing Hospital in America*. Nashville: Baptist Healing Hospital Trust, 2010.

Chapman, Erie. *The Caregivers Meditations: Reflections on Loving Presence*. Nashville: October Hill Press, 2007.

Salzberg, Sharon. *The Kindness Handbook: A Practical Companion*. Boulder, CO: Sounds True, 2008.

Salzberg, Sharo. *The Force of Kindness: Change Your Life with Love & Compassion*. Boulder, CO: Sounds True, 2005.

Allen, Paula Gunn. *Off The Reservation: Reflection on Boundary Busting, Border-Crossing Loose Cannons*. Boston: Beacon Press, 1999.

Barks, Coleman. *The Essential Rumi*. New York: HarperOne, 1997.

Milne, A. A. *The Complete Tales of Winnie the Pooh*. New York: Dutton Children's Book, 1994.

Web Resources

For information and updates on the Framingham Heart Study: http://www.framinghamheartstudy.org/index.html

The poet and Rumi interpreter, Coleman Barks: www.colemanbarks.com

A Network for Grateful Living "provides education and support for the practice of grateful living as a global ethic,...Gratefulness...is a universal practice that fosters personal transformation, cross-cultural understanding, interfaith dialogue, intergenerational respect, nonviolent conflict resolution, and ecological sustainability." http://www.gratefulness.org/a/index.htm

Healthy Caregiving offers information to caregivers so they may practice authentic sustainable self-care: http://www.healthycaregiving.com/pages/mission.html

Compassion Fatigue Awareness Project. www.compassionfatigue.org

Inspired by Ben's bells, kindness charms are being hung in Sedona. http://kindnesscharms.blogspot.ca

"Beholden to no influence, partiality or structures of power, the award (the Peace Prize) is to be accessible to people of all socioeconomic stations, affiliations and localities,..." The intention is, "to applaud the recipients' exceptional contributions to the advancement of greater goodwill, peace, compassion, kindness and safety in the world." www.peaceprize.com

The extraordinary singer/songwriter Tracy Chapman.
www.tracychapman.com

"The Forgiveness Project is a UK based charity that uses storytelling to explore how ideas around forgiveness, reconciliation and conflict resolution can be used to impact positively on people's lives, through the personal testimonies of both victims and perpetrators of crime and violence. www.theforgivenessproject.com

Index

A
affection, 52, 70, 166, 245
Alcoholic Anonymous,
Allen, Paula Gunn, 223
all my relations, 166
altruism, 56-57, 65-66, 70, 176
angels, 126, 174
Anglican, 154,
animals, 73, 89, 96
Aquinas, Thomas, 66, 165
Aristotle, 195
Armstrong, Karen, 36
attitude, 87, 100, 141, 143
avocation, 152-56, 162, 222, 226,

B
baby, 147, 209, 255
beginner's mind, 157-159
beliefs, 26-28, 30-32, 40, 135, 158, 238
belonging, 59, 166-67, 172, 174, 178-79, 180-181, 187, 192, 196, 199, 218
Brain, 65, 69, 156
brave, 90, 210
breathe, 98, 156, 185, 257
Brooks, Arthur C., 55

Brooks, Rod, 182
Buddhist, 27, 158
Buddhism, 32
Buscaglia, Leo, 162

C
Cancer, 138, 159-60, 196, 209, 218, 225, 228, 231, 238, 239, 247
career, 99, 113-15, 141, 148-49, 209, 218, 225, 228, 231, 239, 243, 247, 151
Catholic, 67, 136
CCARE, 56-57
change, 35, 39, 45, 72, 82, 84-86, 88-89, 93, 103, 120-22, 134, 157, 173, 178, 212, 219, 220
Chapman, Erie, 239, 350
Chapman, Tracy, 173
charity, 60, 153, 178, 180
Charter for Compassion, 36-39, 176
children, 38-39, 58, 63, 72-73, 89, 134-35, 144, 156, 168, 178, 179, 181, 192, 203, 208-09
Christmas, 184
citizens, 53-54, 177, 180
civic leaders, 174, 177-78

Clapham, Ward, 105, 172
coffee, 111, 211-14, 240
colleagues, 29, 31, 65, 105, 171, 173, 221, 242, 251
Community, 27, 34, 38, 52, 88-89, 101, 106, 108, 110, 185, 195, 197, 200, 215, 242
Compassion Action Network, 176
compassion fatigue, 214, 222, 208
compassion lab, 218
connection, 65-69, 94, 132,170, 174, 179, 180, 188, 197, 198
contemplative, 35, 44-46, 70, 206
cooperation, 73
cortisol, 69
co-workers, 31, 171, 196
culture, 14,30-34, 98, 176
customer, 1`7, 71, 143, 140, 141, 245
crime,108, 193,

D

Dalai Lama Center for Peace and Education, 26, 58
darkness,60, 81-82, 97, 192
Darwin, 56, 74
devotion, 21, 25, 30-31, 35-36, 39, 44-47, 62, 72,183, 206, 209, 257
de Waal, Frans, 73
dichotomy, 80-82, 181
disability,24, 47, 156, 173, 214
dog, 9, 73, 204
donation, 54-55
Doty, James, Dr., 56
dream, 82, 141, 143, 163
Dutton, Jane, Dr., 218

E

education, 56, 63, 174, 176, 177, 225
Egyptian village, 91
Einstein, Albert, 49, 51-52
elderly, 79, 138, 226
elephant, 73
Emerson, Ralph Waldo, 65, 98, 129
Emory University, 15

empathy, 38, 57-58, 62, 65-67, 93, 109, 183, 192, 201, 241,
employees, 10, 100

F

Facebook, 179, 183
faculty, 120, 142
faith, 26, 32, 44, 60, 112, 137, 144, 165, 177, 249
family, 14, 28, 31, 35-35, 42, 60, 79, 97, 101, 126, 134, 138, 139, 143, 150, 152, 155, 157, 168, 169, 170-71, 173, 181, 184, 198, 204, 208, 214, 216, 218, 219, 221, 222, 227, 229, 230, 233, 242, 246, 247
flowers, 79, 80, 145-46
forgiveness, 159
Framingham, 220
Fraser Institute, 54
Free the Children, 167, 178-79, 180-81,
friends, 7, 44, 47, 73, 77, 116, 126, 134, 181, 184, 188, 195, 208, 221, 227, 241, 242
Frost, Robert, 157

G

Generosity Index, 54
global, 18, 31, 36, 38, 39, 56, 59, 176, 178, 180-81, 182-83, 208
Golden Rule, 30-40, 42-45
good samaritan, 247, 248, 249
Gottman, John, Dr., 104-105
grace, 15, 31, 146, 240
Greater Good Science Center, 57
grief, 35, 65, 147, 192, 237

H

happy, 26-27, 54, 62, 72-73, 79-80, 84, 91, 93, 102, 109-100, 112, 129, 136, 196, 221, 230
happiness, 35, 57, 62, 64, 71, 101,

117-118, 139, 221, 251
harmony, 101
health, 52, 59, 61-62, 85, 87, 136, 147, 149, 198, 199, 207, 209, 211, 214, 215, 222, 242, 245
healthcare, 5-9, 14, 57, 151, 209, 216, 242
heard, 8, 108, 126-127, 158, 170, 197, 241, 242, 230, 237, 239, 250
heart, 13-18, 29, 37, 39, 45-47, 61, 63, 69, 93-95, 125-127, 136-138, 143, 144, 147, 152, 170, 190, 191-92, 198, 200, 207-08, 213, 214, 220, 223-24, 225, 228-30, 232, 235, 240, 257
heartbeat, 166
helpers high, 59, 61, 64
homeless, 184, 185, 186, 256
hope, 18, 29, 45, 52, 60, 78-83, 92, 94, 109, 119, 166, 168, 172, 178, 193, 220, 228
hormone, 67-69
hospital, 6-7, 79, 88, 94-95, 112, 134, 135, 147, 160, 240, 244, 245, 225
house, 42, 145-146, 191, 216, 223-24, 225, 230
Human Resources, 40, 119, 214, 225
humanity, 18, 28, 37-38, 65, 148, 172, 231, 240

I

inclusion, 51, 172, 178
India, 4, 14, 59, 144, 145, 161, 219, 239
insurance, 100, 143, 182, 208
intention, 41, 71, 86, 144, 148, 214, 222
interconnectedness, 178, 180, 192
interfaith, 32
isolation, 109, 193, 195, 204

J

joy, 35, 59, 66, 110, 125, 143-44, 222, 224, 238, 239
Judaism, 28, 30, 33

K

kindness, 5, 9, 32, 35, 39, 46, 82, 110, 143, 153, 172, 169, 197, 210, 217, 233, 242, 257-58
King Martin Luther, Jr., 49, 155
Kentucky, 26, 58, 174-75

L

Lama, Dalai, 26, 58
light, 5, 41, 64, 81-82, 94, 97, 100-114, 235
Lincoln, Abraham, 12,
listening, 113, 121, 127, 142, 162-63, 210, 227, 235, 236, 238, 239, 242-44, 246, 257, 258
loneliness, 195
Losada, Marcial, Dr., 102
love, 4, 25, 35, 38, 74, 79, 95, 101, 125, 140, 141, 148, 155-60, 166, 197, 204, 206, 211, 217, 228, 229, 231, 235, 243, 246, 251
Luks, Allan , 59
Lyubomirsky, Sonja, Dr, 86, 101

M

marketers, 183
marriage, 23, 92, 94, 104
Marshall, Joseph, 39-40
Masai, 179
mayor, 174-75, 177
meaning, 15, 17, 25, 47, 67, 73, 142-143-44, 154, 157
meditation, 11, 67, 70, 158
mindfulness, 47, 57, 240
money, 41, 53, 55, 72, 153, 181, 184-87, 196
Mongrain, Myriam, Dr., 61-62
Morocco, 14, 28, 208, 219
Mother Placid, 3, 12-15
Mother Teresa, 3, 131, 136-137, 139,

147-48, 161, 255
movement, 32-36, 39, 56, 178, 194, 258
Musick, Marc Dr., 63, 223

N
Native American, 28, 39
nature, 4, 43, 46, 52, 70, 83, 94, 96
neighbor, 70, 187-88, 197, 224
Nurse, 94-95. 137, 149, 225, 230, 240, 243, 244, 250

O
O'Donohue, John, 241
optimistic, 99-101, 108-111, 113, 120-124, 143
oxytocin, 67-70, 123, 143

P
parents, 24, 44, 72-73, 89, 230
Peacefulness, 101
Picoult, Jody, 209
positive psychology 84, 91
Positive Tickets, 105-08, 172
Post, Stephen, Dr., 66
presence, 18, 41, 43, 44, 46, 70, 143-144, 201, 207-09, 217, 222, 226, 228, 230, 232, 234, 235, 237, 240-41, 246, 247, 249, 251, 257
Princeton, 248
productivity, 101-03, 214-15

R
reciprocity, 34-35, 64, 127, 140, 183
recruitment, 99
retention, 99
Riessman, Frank Dr., 64
right action, 166, 186, 189, 190, 200
Royal Canadian Mounted Police, 105
Rumi, 123-124, 223, 241

S
sacred, 30, 194, 205, 207
safe, 15, 98
School, 23, 27, 31, 45, 46, 106-107, 126, 140, 152, 167, 178, 200, 206, 226
science, 22, 49, 51, 59, 66-67, 68, 85, 118, 123, 127, 181, 203, 206
Seligman, Martin, Dr., 84, 100
service, 16-17, 27, 39-40, 42, 60, 65-66, 71, 95, 107, 156, 173, 175, 176, 192, 198, 220, 223, 245,
smile, 5, 25,29, 53, 60, 66, 72, 80, 95-6, 107, 126, 162, 166, 171, 179, 178, 186, 192, 226, 228
social worker, 147-48
spiritual, 18, 24, 26, 27, 37, 52, 59, 156, 214
Stanford University, 56
Stony Brook University, 57, 66
suffering, 13, 26, 37-38, 59, 72 77, 97, 136, 171, 192, 204, 208, 223, 229, 231, 240
Sufi, 223, 241,
survival, 63, 74, 89
sustainable, 148, 176

T
Talmud, 31, 33
tasks, 17, 152, 154, 133-35, 136, 137, 140- 41, 144, 148, 241
Theologian, 223
Three-Second-Pause, 239-41, 250, 256
toilets,133, 135-36, 139, 146, 147, 161
touch, 63, 66, 71, 113, 122, 127, 162, 171, 208, 251
trauma, 191-92, 230, 237
treasures, 45, 204, 208, 251,
Tutu, Desmond, 165, 166

U
unconditional, 47, 125, 157
universe, 43, 51, 81

university, 55, 61, 62-63, 65, 66-68,
    85, 142, 176, 181, 218, 230
University of California, 57, 117
University of Michigan, 218, 230
University of Washington, 104

V

Valentine's Day, 110-112, 143
values, 18, 26, 40, 87. 142, 153, 183,
    198, 235, 238, 244
verb, 11, 28-29, 51
vocation, 152-154, 155, 156, 162, 198
volunteer, 175, 180, 197, 198, 203,
    219, 226, 243
Vonnegut, Kurt, 195
vow, 25

W

war, 25, 91, 193-94, 203
Winnie the Pooh, 251
We Day, 180-81
work, 5-9, 12, 14, 17, 24-25, 31, 37,
    41, 43, 47, 52-59, 63-68, 73,
    81-84, 99-105, 109, 111, 119,
    120-21, 125, 133-38, 140-44,
    145, 152, 153,-56, 161, 163,
    169-73, 175, 185-87, 190, 196-
    98, 206-08, 211, 214,-19, 224-
    25, 227, 230, 242, 245
World Giving Index, 53-55
worship, 39, 44

Y

Youngson, Robin, Dr., 243, 247
YouTube, 73, 183
York University, 61

Z

Zak, Dr. Paul J., 68-69, 71

With Gratitude

This is the enjoyable piece at the conclusion of writing a book. The part where you get to acknowledge the very people who made your words come to life with their infinite patience, generous talents, and unconditional support. When you begin to write a book of this magnitude the process becomes all-consuming, making your life suddenly take a turn; you can get lost easily and need wise people, committed to the essence of the vision, to ensure the book will come to fruition the way it was intended. I have been blessed to have those exact people warmly surround me. They have offered up unwavering commitment to place this book in your hands.

It is with the greatest of gratitude I express my appreciation to:

Leslie Nolin, my publisher, my dearest friend, my greatest champion. This book has been a labor of love we both wanted to create. Leslie is a woman of outstanding courage whose life is a woven tapestry of compassion to others. Never has there been a moment when I didn't feel her encouraging presence throughout my day. What I so adore about Leslie is she never doubted my ability to complete, what some days felt like an impossibility, this book. You can keep on writing when you know you have an enduring eminence supporting you unconditionally. She expected me to bring my whole self to the book—it was non-optional—and when I didn't, she encouraged me to go back and tell my story again, and then again. There are no words I can put on this page that will ever fully express my gratitude for her believing in me, endlessly, for the last ten years.

Mary Ann Thompson, my substantive editor extraordinaire. Due to the special nature of this book, we went looking for an editor with unique storytelling talents and were blessed to have found her. Mary Ann's mastery of her craft to uncover the truth hidden in a story is profound. Her ability to draw out the best in my writing and voice has been an amazing experience for me and I have learned so much from her. Mary Ann's sense of humor, passion for perfection, and her deeply committed willingness to go the distance with me to ensure we honored each story in a meaningful way, became a priceless gift to me.

My heartfelt appreciation to the untold number of contributors who submitted their written stories, agreed to be interviewed, or whose lives crossed my path in a variety of ways. Your authenticity to share your innermost thoughts with me has granted me the gift to see compassion through your eyes. When you spend as much time with each story as I have they are no longer flat words on a page. These stories are very much alive and breathing as though the contributors are speaking them firsthand. I am so humbled by your generosity, open hearts, and your willingness to share your profoundly touching life experiences for myself and our readers to witness and learn from you.

To my family and friends who, without upset, unanimously supported my many moments of absenteeism from their lives during this year-long interval of writing. I am forever grateful for your love and support.

About the Author

National Human Resources Expert, Leadership Facilitator and Change Agent

Jaime Kowal

With 30 years in business management, Olivia's career has also included over two decades in Human Resource management and leadership development.

Her approach to people management is as innovative as it is creative. Combine that with her philosophical mind and her vast library of experiences and you have a unique blend of inspiring leadership. Her diverse background included progressive careers in retail and tourism prior to establishing a name in the financial industry as the 'Human Touch' HR Director. It was here she pioneered and spearheaded the implementation of numerous innovative workplace wellness and employee engagement initiatives with outstanding results. Ms. McIvor has worked with hundreds of clients in a broad array of industries including: Healthcare, Technology, Education, Retail, Oil and Gas, Utilities, Natural Resources, Tourism, Hospitality, Financial, and Manufacturing.

In 2000 Olivia ventured into the Entrepreneur world herself as the owner of a unique bookstore devoted to Personal and Professional Leadership. In 2001 Olivia was nominated Female Entrepreneur of the Year by Working Women Magazine and has been featured on the Knowledge Network/Discovery Channel for a segment on workplace wellness.

Ms. McIvor is a senior partner with The Organizational Culture Group Ltd. where her culture enhancement programs have contributed to strengthening leaders across North America. Her **Contagious Kindness** and **Compassion in Action** culture change programs are licensed in five Canadian health care regions to support respectful collegial relationships and enhance compassionate client care.

Ms. McIvor's keynote addresses, consulting and facilitation skills have graced associations, foundations and corporations on topics including **Four Generations-One Workplace, The Business of Kindness, Building Collaborative Relationships, and Compassion in Action.**

Her insight, knowledge and genuine care for workplace culture challenges are forefront in her books, *The Business of Kindness; Creating Work Environments Where People Thrive*, *Four Generations, One Workplace; Sharing in the Information Age* and *Turning Compassion into Action: A Movement Toward Taking Responsibility*. She is also the author and creator of numerous personal and professional development tools.

Ms. McIvor teaches in the Faculty of Business at the British Columbia Institute of Technology (BCIT). She contributes to her community as she serves on the board of the Kindness Foundation of Canada as well as the Greater Vancouver Compassionate Network.

Ms. McIvor lives in Vancouver, Canada

Contact Ms. McIvor

To inquire regarding a speaking engagements please email requests to: info@OLIVIAMCIVOR.com

Visit her professional Website: OLIVIAMCIVOR.com or

Corporate Website: Organizationalculturegroup.com

For daily inspirational messages join her followers on Facebook: Facebook/OliviaMcIvor

Ms. McIvor's Products can be ordered through: FairWinds-press.com

<u>**Quantity Orders:**</u> Should you wish to a order larger quantity of products for conferences, company learning, staff or teams development please call: 604-913-0649 for discount information.